T0274694

BATTLEFIELDS

PAST AND PRESENT

Thunder Bay Press
An imprint of Printers Row Publishing Group
9717 Pacific Heights Blvd, San Diego, CA 92121
www.thunderbaybooks.com • mail@thunderbaybooks.com

Copyright © 2023 Quarto Publishing plc

All rights reserved. No part of this publication may be reproduced, distributed, or transmitted in any form or by any means, including photocopying, recording, or other electronic or mechanical methods, without the prior written permission of the publisher, except in the case of brief quotations embodied in critical reviews and certain other noncommercial uses permitted by copyright law.

Printers Row Publishing Group is a division of Readerlink Distribution Services, LLC.

Thunder Bay Press is a registered trademark of Readerlink Distribution Services, LLC.

Correspondence regarding the content of this book should be sent to Thunder Bay Press, Editorial Department, at the above address. All other inquiries should be addressed to The Bright Press at the address below.

Thunder Bay Press
Publisher: Peter Norton
Associate Publisher: Ana Parker
Editor: Dan Mansfield

This book was conceived, designed, and produced by
The Bright Press, an imprint of the Quarto Group,
1 Triptych Place, London SE1 9SH,
United Kingdom.
www.quarto.com

The Bright Press
Publisher: James Evans
Editorial Director: Isheeta Mustafi
Art Director: James Lawrence
Managing Editor: Jacqui Sayers
Senior Editor: Dee Costello
Project Editor: Anna Southgate
Senior Designer: Emily Nazer
Design: JC Lanaway
Picture Research: Jenny Quiggin and Jane Lanaway
Text: Peter Darman

Library of Congress Cataloging-in-Publication data available on request.

ISBN: 978-1-6672-0515-1

Printed in Malaysia

27 26 25 24 23   1 2 3 4 5

Cover credits

Front cover: Alamy/Artokoloro (past); Shutterstock/aneta.las (present).

Back cover: Alamy/Everett Collection Historical (top left); Getty Images/Bettmann (center, top right); iStock/Eloi_Omella (top right); Library of Congress, Washington DC (bottom left); Shutterstock/Ken Felepchuk (center, bottom left); Shutterstock/JamesChen (bottom right); Shutterstock/Nick Martinson: (center, bottom right).

BATTLEFIELDS

PAST AND PRESENT

THUNDER BAY
P·R·E·S·S
San Diego, California

CONTENTS

INTRODUCTION

PAST AND PRESENT Taking you on an exhilarating journey through time, *Battlefields Past and Present* explores the sites of the most famous military clashes fought in the nineteenth and twentieth centuries, and reveals how they look today.

Battlefields are immortal, in that the ground they were fought on is extant forever. It can be plowed, altered, and built on, but will always be the place where armies clashed and soldiers died on a specific day in the past. Featuring more than fifty battlefields from five major wars of the last 200 years—the American Civil War, World Wars I and II, the Korean War, and the Vietnam War—this book places past and present photographs side by side to reveal how the sites have changed over time. Discover how battlefields of the American Civil War are being returned to the state they were in when Union and Confederate soldiers marched across them. Marvel at the ways in which the cities of Europe and Japan almost completely destroyed in World War II have been rebuilt. And visit the many sacred memorials that have been erected in honor of those who have fallen.

▶ **Past and present photographs help to conjure the spirit of the battlefields more closely, and to show how they have been immortalized over the years. Here, photographs of the Champs Élysées—one in August 1944 and the other today—show how little the street has changed.**

The historic photographs in this book are genuine and the imperfections of their age only add to the richness of the stories they tell.

1861—1865

AMERICAN CIVIL WAR

FIRST BULL RUN

MANASSAS, VIRGINIA, JULY 1861

◀ After crossing Bull Run, a stream flowing through the battlefield, Union flanking forces forded the Catharpin Run at Sudley Springs Ford. This photograph was taken after the battle and shows Union cavalry on the other side of the ford. During the battle, more than 13,000 Union soldiers passed over this spot.

▲ The Sudley Springs Ford wayside marker today. The image gives a good impression of how the terrain would have looked on July 21, 1861. Conditions were hot and dusty, and many men fell out to fill canteens with muddy water. They also threw away unnecessary equipment to lighten loads.

The First Battle of Bull Run was the Civil War's initial major conflict. On July 21, 1861, with Union and Confederate armies gathered between their opposing capitals (Washington and Richmond), Union General Irvin McDowell advanced and ran into Confederate General Pierre Beauregard at Bull Run, unaware that Beauregard's 20,000 men were expecting reinforcements of around 12,000. Of McDowell's 28,000 soldiers, only 2,000 were professional. McDowell tried to outflank the Confederates, but after an initial advance, his forces were checked by the stand of Brigadier General Thomas Jackson's Virginia Brigade, earning Jackson the nickname "Stonewall." Seeing the Confederate reinforcements, the Union army fled in panic. Union losses were 2,706 compared to Confederate casualties of 1,981. Only the actions of professional Union troops in the rearguard prevented McDowell's army from destruction as it fled back to Washington. The Confederates did not pursue, a decision that was soon to prove a mistake.

- This is the so-called Stone House, located near the intersection of the Warrenton Turnpike and Sudley Road on the First Bull Run battlefield. Because it was located at a crossroads, it was fought over in two battles during the Civil War. After the First Bull Run, the house filled with wounded Union soldiers captured following the Confederate victory.

- The Stone House is now part of Manassas National Battlefield Park (the First Battle of Bull Run is also known as the First Battle of Manassas). During the second battle here, in August 1862, the Confederates shelled the house with artillery. Since its acquisition by the U.S. National Park Service, both the building and its surrounding landscape have been restored to their Civil War–era appearance.

RICHMOND
VIRGINIA, JULY–AUGUST 1862

Only 95 miles separated Washington from the Confederate capital of Richmond. In 1862, the commander of the Union army, General George B. McClellan, moved his men south to threaten Richmond. If the city fell, the war would be over. Opposing him was General Robert E. Lee. The action resulted in the Seven Days' Battles (June 25–July 1) to the north and east of Richmond, which beat off McClellan's offensive. It would be two years before Richmond would be threatened again. Richmond was not only the Confederate capital, it was also a rail hub, a center of industry, and the location of the large Tredegar Iron Works that produced rail tracks and artillery. Not a particularly large city, its population at the beginning of the Civil War was 38,000, including 11,739 slaves.

However, after the outbreak of hostilities, the population rose rapidly as soldiers, laborers, bureaucrats, and speculators poured into the city, swelling its numbers to 100,000 in 1863 and to a population between 130,000 and 150,000 by the end of the war in 1865. The Confederacy might have won at First Bull Run and Seven Days', but the consequence of these actions meant Richmond was flooded with casualties. One treatment center, Chimborazo Hospital, alone treated 78,000 patients during the war.

◀ **A burned-out Richmond following the so-called Evacuation Fire in April 1865. Following Lee's failed attempts to relieve the city toward the end of the war, President Jefferson Davis ordered its evacuation. Before they left, Confederate officers set fire to tobacco warehouses. The fire spread, destroying up to 1,000 buildings, although the capitol was preserved from the flames.**

▲ **Today, the capitol is surrounded by skyscrapers and barely visible. It was designed by Thomas Jefferson in 1785 and was the first building in the United States to be constructed in the form of an ancient Roman temple. After the Civil War, it became a Union army headquarters.**

ANTIETAM

MARYLAND, SEPTEMBER 1862

In early 1862, General Lee crossed the Potomac River to invade Union-held Maryland. His objective was to encourage Britain and France to recognize, and then assist, the Confederacy. Lee had 55,000 men, McClellan 97,000. After two weeks of maneuvering, the two sides clashed at Antietam Creek on September 17. McClellan tried to roll up Lee's left flank with three corps, but the attack degenerated into a series of uncoordinated assaults, the costliest of which occurred in "Bloody Lane." By the end of the battle, the Union had suffered 12,400 casualties, the Confederates 13,700. The stalemate was the bloodiest one-day battle of the war and a strategic defeat for the Confederacy, Lee's invasion having failed.

◀ Top: Union reserve artillery near McClellan's headquarters at Pry House, behind the central portion of the battlefield. McClellan and his staff officers watched the battle from the front lawn of the house. Bottom: Today, the cornfields are much as they were during the attack. The battle lasted nearly three hours as both sides fed troops into the cornfield. Almost 8,000 Union and Confederate soldiers were killed or wounded in the cornfield at Antietam.

▶ Top: Lower Bridge, the crossing over Antietam Creek, was in the southern sector of the battlefield. General Robert Toombs and 500 Confederates held the bridge against three Union assaults launched by General Burnside's corps. Toombs abandoned the bridge at 1:00 p.m., allowing time for Confederate reinforcements to reach the battlefield. Bottom: The bridge as it appears today, fully restored to how it would have looked during the Civil War.

FREDERICKSBURG
VIRGINIA, DECEMBER 1862

Under pressure from President Lincoln, the new commander of the Army of the Potomac, General Ambrose Burnside, devised a plan to cross the Rappahannock River and advance on Richmond to beat General Lee to the Confederate capital. The place Burnside chose to cross the Rappahannock was at the town of Fredericksburg. The bridges over the river had been destroyed, which meant Burnside had to wait for pontoon bridges to arrive. This gave the Confederates time to prepare their defenses. When the battle began on December 11, Union soldiers crossed the river and occupied the town. But assaults against Marye's Heights on December 13 incurred heavy losses and two days later Burnside withdrew the Army of the Potomac back across the Rappahannock.

▼ **Fredericksburg, as Union soldiers would have seen it on their approach in December 1862, the bridges across the river having been destroyed. Supported by more than 140 cannons on the northern bank, Union engineers began to lay down pontoon bridges across the river. Their fire inflicted tremendous damage on the town. Marye's Heights lay beyond.**

▶ **Fredericksburg today. The rail bridge across the Rappahannock River was destroyed twice during the Civil War, first by the Confederates as they retreated from Manassas to Richmond in March 1862, and then by Union forces after they had rebuilt it during their occupation of the town in May 1862. At the time of the Civil War, there was far less foliage on the riverbanks.**

JACKSON AT FREDERICKSBURG

On the right of the Confederate line, 60,000 Union soldiers attacked General Thomas "Stonewall" Jackson's corps (34,000) and pushed it back. Only a series of desperate counterattacks prevented a rout. In stark contrast to Marye's Heights, the Confederates suffered heavy casualties in the fighting. On the heights, successive Union attacks were easily defeated by Confederate forces behind a stonewall. But Jackson's position was very different, his soldiers facing a wide-open plain extending to the river and covered by Union artillery across the river.

▶ **Fairfield House, ten miles south of Fredericksburg, where General Jackson was taken after being wounded by friendly fire at the Battle of Chancellorsville in 1863. After having his left arm amputated, Jackson was to be transported by rail to Richmond but died beforehand. Today, the house is a historic site, open to the public.**

▲ **"Stonewall" Jackson was a deeply religious man. He often rode with his left arm in the air, claiming it aided his circulation. He was Lee's right-hand man until his death at Chancellorsville in May 1863.**

GETTYSBURG
PENNSYLVANIA, JULY 1863

The Battle of Gettysburg, July 1–3, 1863, was the pivotal clash of Lee's second invasion of the North. On July 1, Confederate forces were victorious, but Union commander General George Meade was able to establish defensive positions south of the town, on Culp's Hill and Cemetery Ridge. On July 2, the Confederates failed to take Little Round Top in the south of the Union position and a bloody stalemate ensued. Lee launched an attack against the center of Meade's position on July 3. Some 15,000 troops were massed on Seminary Ridge for an attack on Cemetery Ridge, half a mile away. The Confederate attack reached Union positions on Cemetery Ridge, but was quickly repulsed. The failure signaled the end of the battle and a Union victory, though at a cost of 3,155 dead and 14,529 wounded. Confederate losses were 3,903 dead and 18,735 wounded.

◀ The summit of Little Round Top, the left flank of the Union position. Though overshadowed by its larger neighbor, Big Round Top, it was more important because it had been cleared of trees and could accommodate more soldiers.

▲ A bronze statue of Brigadier General Gouverneur K. Warren on Little Round Top, erected in 1888. When he discovered the hill was almost empty of troops on July 2, on his own authority he diverted troops to the position and thus arguably saved the Union army from disaster.

LITTLE ROUND TOP A hill at the southern end of the Union battle line, Little Round Top had been cleared of trees, giving excellent views of Confederate troops attacking from the west. Lee believed that, if he could take Little Round Top, the Confederates could roll up the entire Union battle line. On July 2, due to a mix-up, the hill was largely empty of Union soldiers. However, Meade sent Brigadier General Gouverneur K. Warren to assess the situation. Warren saw the danger and quickly called for reinforcements, thus saving the day and winning the battle.

▲ Major General Gouverneur K. Warren

◀ The battle-scarred Evergreen Cemetery Gatehouse, photographed after the battle. During the battle, the gatehouse was the headquarters of the commander of the Union XI Corps, General Oliver O. Howard.

▼ The gatehouse's two brick towers support a memorial arch. The structure was repaired in 1885 and the adjoining lodge, seen on the right, was built. The gatehouse gives access to the cemetery, where more than 10,000 graves are located.

EVERGREEN CEMETERY

Established in 1854, the Evergreen Cemetery was the scene of heavy fighting on July 2. Located just south of the town of Gettysburg, the cemetery served as an artillery platform for Union cannons during the battle. Toward the end of fighting, the Confederates attacked the batteries of the Union XI Corps but were beaten off, some Union soldiers using gravestones for cover during an hour of bitter fighting.

◀ Culp's Hill in 1863, photographed after the battle. In the foreground are earth entrenchments, called "lunettes," from where Union cannons fired on the Confederates as they attacked. The bullet-shredded trees in the background attracted tourists for decades afterward.

▼ Monument to the 4th Ohio Volunteer Infantry Regiment, on East Cemetery Hill. On July 2, Union artillery on East Cemetery Hill and Culp's Hill combined to disable fourteen Confederate cannons based on Benner's Hill, a short distance to the east.

CULP'S HILL An important site on the right flank of the Union position at Gettysburg, Culp's Hill was occupied throughout the three-day battle, the Union having built trenches and breastworks to turn it into a very strong defensive position. On July 3, 22,000 Union and Confederate soldiers battled for control of the hill, the Confederates withdrawing after six hours of fighting, having suffered heavy casualties.

SPOTSYLVANIA COURT HOUSE

VIRGINIA, MAY 1864

A key road junction on the way to Richmond, in the summer of 1864, Spotsylvania Court House became the objective of the Union Army of the Potomac. The Federal commander, General Ulysses S. Grant, began moving 101,000 troops toward it on May 7, only to be blocked by the quick reaction of General Robert E. Lee and his 56,000-man Army of Northern Virginia. Thus began a major battle commencing on May 8, Union assaults foundering against strong Confederate entrenchments. The fighting continued until May 21, by which time Grant had lost 18,400 dead and Lee 12,687. Neither side had achieved victory.

▲ **Spotsylvania Court House, photographed after the battle, showing the extensive damage done to the building as a result of the vicious fighting that took place around it. One eyewitness recorded: "some shot through by cannonballs, some with arms and legs knocked off, and some with their heads crushed in by the fatal fragment of exploding shells."**

◀ **Today, a fully restored courthouse stands in the same spot, having been redesigned in 1901.**

◀ **General Grant's council of war at Massaponax Church, near Spotsylvania Court House, Virginia, on May 21, 1864. He and his senior officers were planning the next phase of the so-called Overland Campaign. Grant, smoking a cigar, is seated on one of the pews that had been removed from the church (second on the left on the bench in front of the trees).**

MASSAPONAX CHURCH Massaponax Baptist Church was used as a headquarters by both Union and Confederate forces during the Civil War. It was also used as a stable and a hospital. After the war ended, the interior walls had to be whitewashed to cover the graffiti and marks left by the soldiers. The church was originally established in 1788, but the original log cabin was demolished and replaced by the brick building that still stands today.

◀ **Union soldiers congregating at the church before the start of the council of war. They are soldiers of the 114th Pennsylvania Regiment, which served as guard at headquarters of the Army of the Potomac.**

◀ **Massaponax Baptist Church is largely unchanged since Civil War times. The brick building was less than ten years old when the war began.**

BATTLE OF THE CRATER

PETERSBURG, VIRGINIA, JULY 1864

In the summer of 1864, General Grant marched the Army of the Potomac east and then south to capture the rail hub of Petersburg, 23 miles south of Richmond. On June 15, Union troops reached Petersburg but were repulsed. More troops from both sides were fed into the battle, which degenerated into prolonged warfare. To break the deadlock, Union miners under Colonel Henry Pleasants tunneled under Confederate entrenchments and planted 8,000 pounds of gunpowder. The mine was exploded at 4:40 a.m. on July 30, creating a crater 170 feet long, 80 feet wide, and 30 feet deep. The division of General James Ledlie was sent in to exploit the breach, but the attack was poorly organized. Some 20,000 Union soldiers became trapped in the crater, where the Confederates slaughtered them. The attack was called off with 3,798 Union casualties. Confederate losses were 1,500.

▲ Lieutenant General Ulysses S. Grant

◀ Top: The mine entrance used by Pleasants and his men to burrow under Confederate entrenchments. Digging began on June 25 and the miners were soon excavating 40 feet a day. The shaft was finished on July 17, with a length of 510 feet. Bottom: The entrance to the mine was out of sight of Confederate lines on the other side of the slight rise in this photograph.

▶ Top: The crater created by the detonation of 8,000 pounds of gunpowder beneath Confederate entrenchments was spectacular in appearance. Due to the timidity of the subsequent Union assault, the Confederates were able to seal the breach and the siege dragged on until April 1865. Bottom: Today, the site of the crater is part of the Petersburg National Battlefield. The well-tended greenery gives little hint of the 70,000 casualties suffered during the siege.

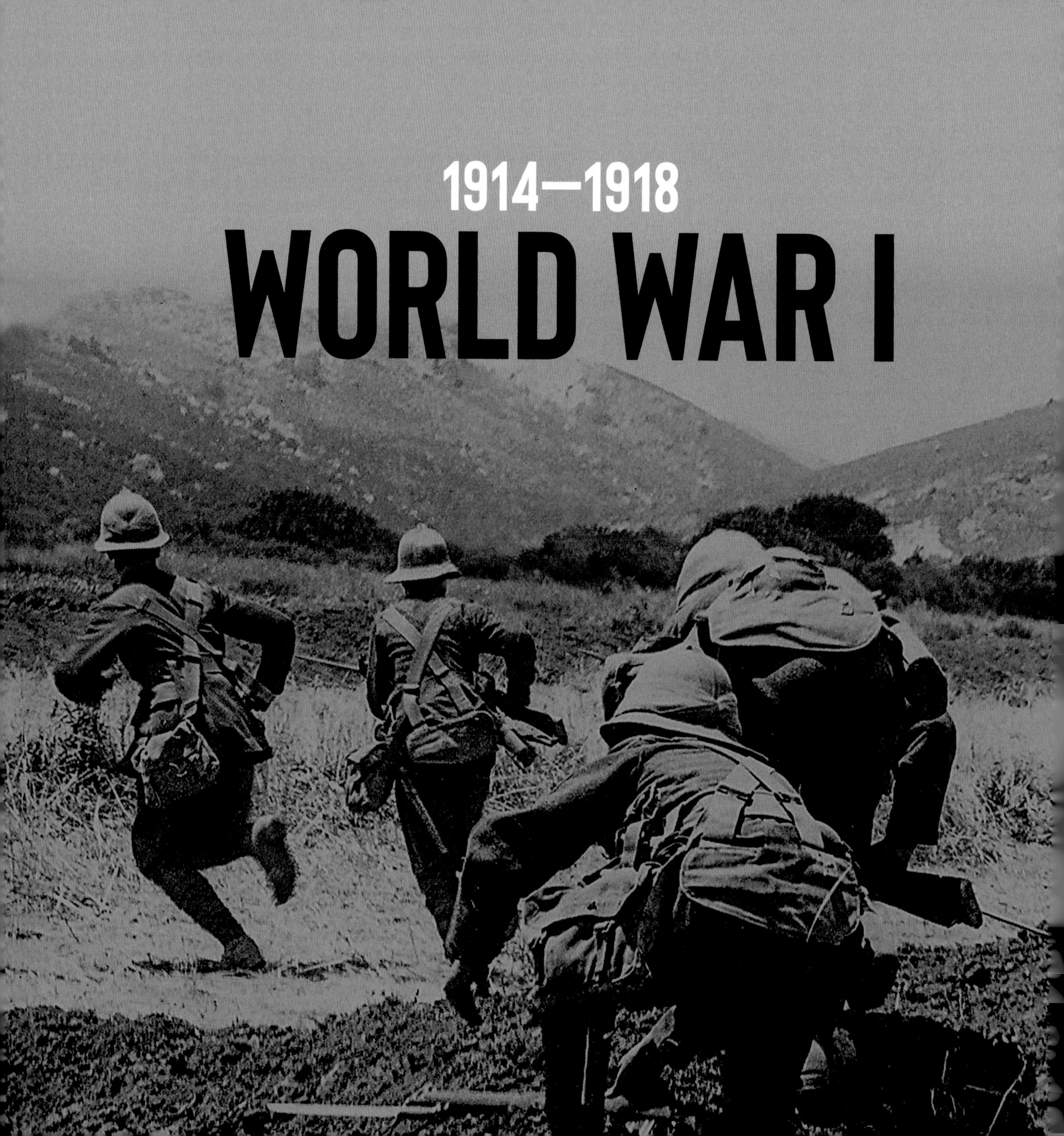

1914—1918
WORLD WAR I

MONS
BELGIUM, AUGUST 1914

When World War I began, the British Expeditionary Force (100,000 men under Sir John French) crossed the English Channel and moved into Belgium. Near the city of Mons, the British were struck by the 1st German Army on August 23. Outnumbered, they put up a stout resistance, the rapid and accurate fire of the British bolt-action rifles inflicting a heavy toll on the German attackers. So intense was the British rifle fire that German commanders believed they were facing machine guns. French was prepared to continue the battle the next day, but the withdrawal of the French 5th Army on his right flank meant he had no choice but to retreat as well. Thus began a two-week retreat from Mons over a distance of 80 miles, fighting a continual rearguard action against the Germans, which included the Battle of Le Cateau, the biggest battle the British Army had fought since Waterloo.

▲ **Troops of A Company, 4th Battalion, Royal Fusiliers, part of the 3rd Division, British Expeditionary Force, resting in the Grand-Place in Mons, in August 1914. During the Battle of Mons, two men from the Royal Fusiliers, Lieutenant Dease and Private Godley, won the Victoria Cross, the first to do so in World War I.**

▶ **Today, the Grand-Place resembles a medieval square with its cobblestones and fifteenth-century town hall, now a historic site. The bell tower was added in the eighteenth century.**

YPRES

BELGIUM, APRIL 1915–1917

The first German offensive of 1915 on the Western Front was launched against the Allied salient at Ypres, Belgium. It was preceded by the first use of poison gas: chlorine, on April 22. There was another gas attack two days later, the British 2nd Army withdrawing to the outskirts of Ypres. The battle continued until May 25, 1915, the British holding the German attacks. However, their poor positions meant they suffered more casualties—60,000 men—compared to German losses of 35,000. This was one of the few instances on the Western Front where the defenders lost more men than the attackers. At the end of July 1917, British Field Marshal Douglas Haig launched his Flanders offensive from Ypres. The British 5th and 2nd Armies attacked the German 4th Army, but became bogged down in muddy conditions following heavy rains. The battle finally ended on November 6, when the village of Passchendaele, less than seven miles from Ypres, was taken. The offensive had cost the British 240,000 casualties. German losses were equally high.

MENIN GATE, YPRES The Menin Gate Memorial to the Missing bears the names of 54,389 men from Britain and the Commonwealth who fell in the Ypres salient before August 16, 1917, and who have no known graves. During the war, British and Commonwealth soldiers marched from Ypres east into the salient along this road, known at the time by its French name Porte de Menin. Many thousands never returned.

◀ **Ypres and the surrounding area were fought over from October 1914 until nearly the end of World War I in 1918. The battles in and around Ypres inflicted a huge amount of damage on the town. As this photograph shows, it was almost totally destroyed during the conflict.**

▶ **Every evening, at 8:00 p.m. precisely, all traffic is stopped on the road passing through the Menin Gate to allow the Last Post Ceremony to take place. The ceremony lasts for thirty minutes—longer if the occasion is to mark Armistice Day (November 11).**

CLOTH HALL, YPRES In medieval times, the Cloth Hall was the commercial heart of the city, where cloth and wool were traded. A series of buildings surrounding a rectangular courtyard, building work began here in 1200 and took 100 years to complete. The belfry is the oldest part of the building, its foundation stone having been laid in 1201 by the Count of Flanders.

▲ **In November 1914, German incendiary shells struck the Cloth Hall, setting it on fire. The wooden-beamed roofs of the hall and scaffolding surrounding the belfry were burned out.**

► **From 1915, Ypres was shelled on a regular basis by long-range German artillery, and by the end of the war the Cloth Hall had been reduced to a ruin. Only a small part of the belfry was left standing by 1918.**

▲ At the end of World War I, Ypres lay in ruins. The first priority was to rebuild the infrastructure to accommodate displaced citizens who had returned to their homes. Restoration of the Cloth Hall did not begin until 1933. The decision was made to restore the hall to match, as closely as possible, its pre-1914 appearance. The work proceeded slowly and was interrupted by five years of German occupation during World War II. It was completed in 1967.

► German chemist Fritz Haber played a major role in developing poison gas in World War I. He observed the first use of his invention at the Battle of Ypres in 1915. For his work on the Western Front, he was awarded the rank of captain by a grateful kaiser.

►► The British responded to the Germans using poison gas by issuing their troops with gas masks. The mask was made of thinly rubberized canvas and was carried in a canvas bag slung over the shoulder.

GALLIPOLI

TURKEY, APRIL 1915

The Allied landings on the Gallipoli Peninsula in April 1915 were designed to open up an aid route to Russia through the Dardanelles. The main landings took place at Cape Helles on the extreme tip of the peninsula. To the north, 16,000 soldiers of the ANZAC (Australian and New Zealand Army Corps) landed at a place nicknamed "Anzac cove," which was unfortunately within range of Turkish artillery. Surrounded by headlands and under constant enemy fire, the cove soon became the site of two field hospitals and a large supply depot. It remained so for eight months until Allied forces were evacuated from the peninsula in January 1916, their objective having failed at a cost of 250,000 casualties.

◀ Supplies are brought ashore at Anzac Cove. On the first day of the landings, April 25, 1915, of the 16,000 Australian and New Zealand troops who landed, more than 2,000 had been killed or wounded by the next morning.

▼ A short beach hemmed in by steep cliffs and hills, Anzac Cove was unsuitable to allow a quick dash inland. Today the cove is a quiet place containing memorials to the Australian, New Zealand, and Turkish soldiers who fell there.

VERDUN
FRANCE, FEBRUARY–DECEMBER 1916

The longest single battle of World War I, fought over 300 days and nights, the Battle of Verdun saw more than 1,000 shells falling on every yard of the battlefield and 770,000 casualties. The German attack on the French army holding the Verdun salient began on February 21, 1916, with a twelve-hour bombardment by 1,400 artillery pieces. The attacks continued until July 11, by which time the French defenders had suffered 315,000 casualties, and the Germans 280,000. Exhausted and demoralized, the Germans fell back when French General Robert Nivelle launched a counterattack on October 24. The fighting raged until December 18, by which time French losses totaled 542,000 to the Germans' 434,000.

◀ The Meuse River runs through Verdun. The town and its surrounding forts were the objective of the German offensive launched in February 1916. Verdun came under heavy artillery bombardment, which destroyed large parts of the town and the quays along the river.

▲ Verdun was fully restored after the war. The cathedral in the top of the picture had been struck by German artillery throughout 1915 and 1916, and required extensive restoration. Work began in 1920 and was not completed until 1936.

SOMME
FRANCE, JULY 1916

The Somme offensive was originally to be a combined French and British affair, but such were France's losses at Verdun that it became a largely British assault. Mounted on a 15-mile front focused on the town of Bapaume, the attack was preceded by a weeklong artillery bombardment of German positions, with more than 1.5 million shells fired. Unfortunately, German troops held well-established trench lines and deep dugouts, which meant the bombardment failed to reduce the enemy's defenses. When British troops attacked on July 1, they advanced into a hail of machine-gun and artillery fire. On this day British losses were 57,470, including 19,240 killed—the deadliest day in British military history. The Allies made some gains, and the Somme witnessed the first use of British tanks on the battlefield, but the offensive did not achieve a breakthrough and petered out on November 18. That said, Germany lost many of its experienced junior leaders in the Somme offensive, never to replace them.

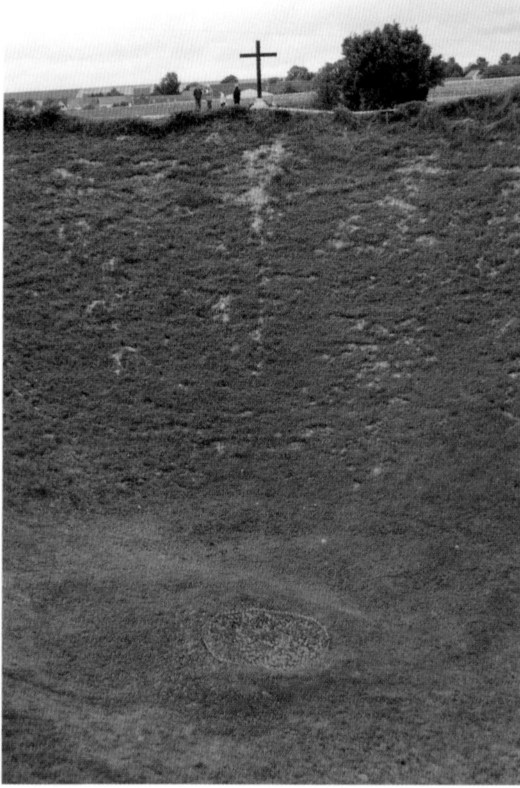

◀◀ Minutes before the start of the Somme offensive, the British set off a mine that demolished a German position known as Schwaben Höhe near La Boisselle, killing many soldiers. However, the Germans reacted with speed, halting the British follow-on attack.

◀ Today, the so-called Lochnagar Crater is the largest manmade crater on earth. It has been maintained due to its historical significance and because it contains undiscovered remains and is such hallowed ground. A wooden cross was placed at the site in 1986.

▲ Soldiers of the South African Brigade were tasked with clearing the Germans from Delville Wood in July 1916. Destroyed by artillery fire, the wood was nothing more than a shell-blasted landscape that filled with mud when it rained. Subjected to incessant German counterattacks, the South Africans were unsuccessful.

◀ Today, the wood is a memorial. The South African government bought the land in 1920 and replanted the trees. Being the final resting place of many South African soldiers, the grounds were otherwise left undisturbed. They retain the original paths through the wood, complete with the remains of shell craters and trenches.

VIMY
FRANCE, APRIL 1917

A prominent ridge 10 miles north of Arras on the Western Front, Vimy Ridge was attacked by the Canadian Corps, part of the British 1st Army, on April 9, 1917. The capture of the ridge was regarded as one of the most successful military operations of World War I. Meticulous planning went into the assault, with models made of the German defenses so officers could familiarize themselves with the battlefield. Hugely symbolic for the Canadian people, the battle was regarded as a milestone in the development of Canada as an independent nation.

◀ **Top: Overlooking the village of Vimy from Vimy Ridge in May 1917, a month after the Canadian assault. Bottom: The same view from the Vimy Memorial, which was built on the highest point of the ridge. The memorial is dedicated to the memory of the 60,000 Canadians who died in France in World War I, particularly the 11,000 who have no known graves, many of whom fell at Vimy Ridge.**

▶ **Top: On July 26, 1936, the memorial was dedicated and the figure of *Canada Bereft* was unveiled by King Edward VIII. Bottom: Carved from a single block of limestone, *Canada Bereft*, also known as *Mother Canada*, symbolizes a young nation grieving its dead in the aftermath of World War I.**

PASSCHENDAELE

BELGIUM, JULY—NOVEMBER 1917

At the end of July 1917, British Field Marshal Douglas Haig launched a new offensive in Flanders, with divisions attacking from the three-year-old Ypres Salient. The advance slowed to a crawl, a result of enemy resistance and the many shell holes created by the ten-day preliminary bombardment filling with water after heavy rains. Fighting continued throughout the fall, the British inching forward in the face of dogged German resistance. On November 6, Commonwealth troops stormed, and held, Passchendaele, a village

less than seven miles from Ypres. It was the final act of a battle that had cost 240,000 British casualties. The Battle of Passchendaele, also known as the Third Battle of Ypres, became synonymous with the futility of many battles fought on the Western Front in World War I, specifically the loss of tens of thousands—sometimes hundreds of thousands—of lives for the gain of a few miles of shell-blasted ground.

◀ **Lying southwest of Passchendaele village, Tyne Cot Cemetery initially contained the bodies of British and Commonwealth soldiers killed in the battle. It was enlarged after the 1918 Armistice, and now contains the graves of 11,954 soldiers, 8,373 of whom remain unidentified.**

▼ **Today, Tyne Cot is the world's largest Commonwealth military cemetery. At the suggestion of King George V, who visited in 1922, a Cross of Sacrifice was erected on the site of one of the German blockhouses that had dominated the ridge during the battle.**

CAMBRAI
FRANCE, NOVEMBER 1917

The British Tank Corps was formed in July 1917. On November 20, 324 British tanks spearheaded an offensive against the German Hindenburg Line southwest of Cambrai, France. The first massed tank assault in history, it punched a six-mile-wide breach in the German defenses. Unfortunately, many tanks broke down and the Germans were able to mass reinforcements on both sides of the British penetration. Ending on December 4, the offensive made no gains in territory, but the use of massed tank formations indicated that the nature of land warfare would soon change forever.

▲ **British soldiers follow a Mark IV tank at Ribécourt-la-Tour near Cambrai. Having a rhomboid shape, caterpillar tracks, and a long body allowed tanks to navigate trenches and craters and smash through barbed wire. Their armor could defeat bullets but was vulnerable to direct hits from artillery.**

▶ **The view from the German-held village of Flesquières toward the woods at Havrincourt. During the Battle of Cambrai, British tanks and infantry advanced up this sunken lane and were struck by small-arms and artillery fire. The infantry withdrew, leaving the tanks isolated. Accurate artillery fire had soon knocked out five tanks and the attack was abandoned.**

◀ Field Marshal Douglas Haig (center) with French prime minister Georges Clemenceau outside the ruins of the German headquarters in Cambrai, October 1918. Canadian troops had entered the city unopposed on October 9.

▼ Left: In retreating from the city, the Germans destroyed what could not be looted and set fire to buildings. Thousands of civilians were made homeless. Right: After the war, Cambrai's town hall was completely restored, along with the cathedral. The authorities had to rebuild half the city's houses due to the German destruction.

MARNE

FRANCE, JULY 1918

The German spring offensive of 1918 was designed to win the war on the Western Front. In May, German troops reached the town of Château-Thierry on the river Marne, just 50 miles from Paris. Their advance was stopped by American machine gunners, who prevented the Germans from crossing the river. In June, the U.S. 2nd Division triumphed in the Battle of Belleau Wood near the town—the first battle of the war fought by U.S. soldiers—and in July the Germans were driven out of Château-Thierry by French and American troops after a four-day battle.

◀ **Two U.S. soldiers in the ruins of Château-Thierry, July 1918. The stone building with the clocktower is the town hall. As can be seen, this part of the town suffered heavy damage during the fighting.**

▲ Alfred von Schlieffen, the German military strategist whose plan to defeat France by a swift encirclement of Paris came to grief at the First Battle of the Marne in 1914. The German 1918 offensive would also come to grief at the Marne, aided in no small measure by the "Doughboys" of the American Expeditionary Force.

▶ Now totally restored, the town hall bears a plaque commemorating American service during World War I. There is also a memorial in the town center, dedicated to the soldiers of the U.S. 3rd Division who defended the town in 1918, and those who fought in Château-Thierry in World War II.

MEUSE-ARGONNE

FRANCE, SEPTEMBER 1918

The Meuse-Argonne offensive announced the arrival of the United States as a major world power. Fighting as an independent force under the command of General John J. Pershing, the U.S. 1st Army began its assault on September 26, 1918, from the Argonne Forest to the Meuse River. More than 1.2 million men were involved in the 47-day offensive. On October 31, the Argonne Forest was cleared of Germans, who were now retreating all along the line (the British and French were also attacking from the west). A final advance began on November 1, and fighting continued until the Armistice on November 11, by which time more than 26,000 Americans had been killed.

▼ **Left: One of the bunkers built for senior German officers in the Argonne Forest. Surrounded by a complex of concrete bunkers, this one was reportedly the headquarters of Crown Prince Wilhelm, the kaiser's son, in 1915. The forest was the scene of heavy fighting in 1914 and 1915, as well as in 1918.**

▼ **Right: U.S. engineers tried to blow up the bunker after it was captured. Explosive charges were placed against the thick concrete wall, but only succeeded in blowing a hole in the ground. Time and nature are now doing what American explosives could not.**

◀ A U.S. infantry gun crew firing a 37mm infantry gun, a French weapon specifically designed to destroy enemy machine-gun nests. Operated by a two-man crew, the weapon could fire up to 35 rounds a minute. Note the helmets, which were similar to those used by the British Army.

◀ Today the Argonne Forest is peaceful and green, though the area is still littered with unexploded ordnance from World War I. Visitors to the area are warned to watch their step when touring bunkers and trench systems.

Built to connect the Somme and Scheldt rivers, the St. Quentin Canal was incorporated within the German Hindenburg Line defenses. Involving British, Australian, and American troops on the right flank of Allied forces, the Battle of St. Quentin Canal began on September 29, 1918. The objective was to break through the heavily defended Hindenburg Line. The assault led to the first full breach of the Hindenburg Line, forcing the Germans out of St. Quentin on October 1. Soldiers of the British North Staffordshire Regiment managed to seize the Riqueval Bridge over the canal before the Germans had a chance to fire their explosive charges positioned on the bridge.

◀ **Opposite: The men who captured the Riqueval Bridge. Soldiers of the British 137th Infantry Brigade (46th Division) are addressed by their commander, Brigadier-General John Vaughan Campbell, at the Riqueval Bridge, October 2, 1918. Left: Today, the canal banks are more overgrown than they were in 1918. The bridge itself is only wide enough for a single vehicle to pass.**

ST. QUENTIN CANAL

FRANCE, SEPTEMBER 1918

STENAY

FRANCE, NOVEMBER 1918

The Armistice that ended the war on the Western Front came into effect at 11:00 a.m. on November 11, 1918. Fighting continued right up until the hour the guns fell silent. The French town of Stenay, on a hill overlooking the river Meuse, was attacked by the U.S. 89th Infantry Division because its commander, General William Wright, wanted his men to take advantage of the town's public bathing facilities! Attacking at 8:00 a.m., the division lost 61 dead and 304 wounded before it captured Stenay. Wright was relieved of command the next day.

◀ **Top: Soldiers of the 89th Division's 353rd Regiment, the unit that captured Stenay in the last U.S. Army action in World War I. Judging by their relaxed demeanor, this photograph was likely taken after the Armistice had come into effect. Bottom: The same Stenay street remains little changed today.**

▶ **Top: Soldiers of the American 353rd Regiment and French civilians celebrate the end of the war on the steps of Stenay's church, November 11, 1918. Most of the fighting had taken place outside the town and resistance inside Stenay was very light. Bottom: Under German occupation since August 1914, Stenay had remained largely unscathed in the conflict. The church, the town's largest building, escaped damage.**

1939—1945
WORLD WAR II

DANZIG

POLAND, SEPTEMBER 1939

After World War I, Danzig, formerly German, became a free city. However, German dictator Adolf Hitler wanted it incorporated into the Third Reich. When German troops attacked Poland on September 1, 1939, Danzig became the scene of the first fighting in World War II. The city was captured despite a heroic Polish defense, and Hitler made a visit on September 19, while fighting was still raging in Poland. At the time, Danzig was inhabited by many Nazi sympathizers, and Hitler received a rapturous reception.

▲ **Hitler enjoys a warm welcome as he is driven through Danzig. The arched structure behind the cavalcade is the Golden Gate, a seventeenth-century building designed by Abraham van den Blocke. The banner in front of it translates as "One People, One Empire, One Leader."**

▶ **Much of Danzig was destroyed during World War II—the result of Allied bombing and Soviet artillery. The Golden Gate was rebuilt in the 1950s, though any trace of German influences were removed, and the city reclaimed its Polish name, Gdansk, as part of the Polish People's Republic (renamed the Republic of Poland after 1989).**

Ein Volk, ein

MAGINOT LINE
FRANCE, MAY 1940

Containing huge forts and garrisoned by 600,000 French troops, the Maginot Line ran along the Franco-German border from Switzerland to Luxembourg. It was not continued along the Franco-Belgian border, however, because French military strategists believed the Germans could not penetrate the Ardennes. When the Germans attacked in the west in May 1940, three panzer corps advanced through the Ardennes, crossed the river Meuse, and progressed rapidly to the English Channel. At a stroke, the extensive defenses of the Maginot Line had become a sideshow in the battle for France.

◀ Adolf Hitler (right) at the Maginot Line in June 1940. At center is General Wilhelm Keitel, Chief of the High Command of the Armed Forces, who described himself as "a loyal shield bearer for Adolf Hitler." He was hanged at Nuremberg in October 1946.

◀▼ Schoenenbourg Fort, part of the Maginot Line defenses. The fort and its defenders saw heavy fighting, as is clear from the damage inflicted on the outside. Between September 1939 and June 1940, it was struck by hundreds of bombs and thousands of artillery rounds.

▶ Behind the forts in the Maginot Line were minefields and tank traps made from iron girders, designed to cripple German armored vehicles. The French did not realize such obstacles could be destroyed by bombers and heavy artillery, or simply bypassed.

▼ The main entrance to Schoenenbourg Fort in northern Alsace. The fort has been open to the public since 1978 and is the largest fort in the Maginot Line that can be visited. Once garrisoned by 650 soldiers, the barracks, kitchens, generating plant, and gun positions can all be toured.

DUNKIRK
FRANCE, JUNE 1940

On May 25, 1940, the British Army was falling back on the Channel port of Dunkirk. The next day, in an operation code-named Dynamo, the British government ordered the Royal Navy to begin the evacuation of troops. However, the port had been under enemy shelling for days and the inner harbor was out of use. The only option was to use the beaches outside Dunkirk. The evacuation was aided by the assistance of "little ships"—hundreds of privately

owned boats that sailed across the English Channel to help pick up men on the beaches and ferry them from shallow waters inshore to larger vessels waiting offshore. Operation Dynamo ended on June 4, by which time 338,226 men had been evacuated from Dunkirk. The price had been high: 243 ships and boats were sunk and the RAF lost 106 aircraft.

◀ **Men on the beaches were exposed to Luftwaffe bombing and strafing, subjecting individuals to immense strain. Sleeplessness and the constant pressure produced a sort of lethargy, except when a boat appeared, which prompted a mad rush into the sea.**

▼ **Though there was no cover on the beaches, the Luftwaffe concentrated its attacks on the large British ships lying offshore. When it did direct its fire against the long lines of troops, the bombs sank deep into the sand, reducing their effect. Greater danger came from the strafing from Stuka dive-bombers.**

CENTER OF DUNKIRK During the fighting in and around Dunkirk in May and June 1940, some 90 percent of the port was destroyed. Pummeled by German artillery and Luftwaffe aircraft, the town and economy were wrecked. The German garrison of "Fortress Dunkirk" surrendered in May 1945, having been besieged since September 1944.

▲ **In the center of the city, the only structure to escape unscathed from the destruction was the bronze statue of the seventeenth-century pirate and French naval commander Jean Bart, erected in 1845.**

◀ **A peaceful and redesigned city square, complete with the Jean Bart statue, in modern-day Dunkirk.**

DUNKIRK TOWN HALL Though large parts of the city, including its town hall, had been destroyed in the fighting, the devastation could have been far worse. Hermann Göring, head of the German Luftwaffe, persuaded Hitler to halt the panzers so his aircraft—500 fighters and 300 bombers—could destroy the Allied forces in the city. Between May 24 and June 4, wave after wave of bombers attacked Dunkirk and the ships offshore, only to encounter RAF fighters that shot down more than 100 Luftwaffe aircraft.

▲ **Built in 1901 in the neo-Flemish style, Dunkirk's town hall was badly damaged in both world wars. By the time of the German surrender in 1945, little more than the 246-foot-tall belfry remained.**

▶ **Dunkirk's town hall today, having been fully restored by 1955. In 1989, the belfry became a UNESCO World Heritage Site. During an annual carnival in the city, the mayor throws smoked herring to the crowd from one of the hall's balconies, a tradition that has roots in the seventeenth century.**

DE PANNE

BELGIUM, MAY–JUNE 1940

De Panne, in Belgium, lies five miles north of Dunkirk. It, too, was used as an evacuation point for Allied troops in May and June 1940. In a desperate measure, makeshift piers were constructed by driving trucks into the sea at low tide and parking them parallel to the beach, to form a pier allowing soldiers to clamber aboard boats that came in at high tide. This work had to be carried out between bouts of enemy shelling and air raids. The village of De Panne fell to the Germans after heavy fighting on June 1.

◀ The scene on De Panne beach following the Germans' capture of the village. Dated June 8, 1940, the image shows the trucks used to speed up evacuations from the beach. By the end of May, embarkation from the beach in daylight was impossible due to enemy fire.

▼ De Panne has the widest beach on Belgium's North Sea coast. Now, among the beach huts and sand dunes, it is difficult to imagine the constant shelling, machine-gun fire, and bombing of 1940.

BATTLE OF BRITAIN

ENGLAND, SEPTEMBER 1940

The Battle of Britain began as a Luftwaffe campaign to disable Britain's Royal Air Force (RAF) and Royal Navy prior to a German invasion of Britain, thus completing the Nazi campaign in the west. The Luftwaffe committed 2,800 aircraft to the campaign, two-thirds of them bombers. In August and early September 1940, the Luftwaffe inflicted serious losses on RAF aircraft, pilots, and bases. But then the German strategy changed. In retaliation for RAF air raids on Berlin, Hitler ordered the Luftwaffe to strike London, thus relieving pressure on RAF airfields as well as factories producing Spitfire and Hurricane fighters. London was bombed but the RAF was saved.

◀▲ Opposite: A German Heinkel He 111 over the Isle of Dogs, London, on September 7, 1940. On that day the docks were hit by 670 tons of high explosives and thousands of incendiaries. Above: The Isle of Dogs today, a center of international finance and luxury residential properties.

◀ Far left: An air-raid warden keeps watch for enemy bombers. Left: RAF pilots rush to their Hurricane fighters during the Battle of Britain. RAF Fighter Command never lost control of the skies over Britain.

LONDON BLITZ

ENGLAND, SEPTEMBER 1940–MAY 1941

Despite losing the Battle of Britain, the Luftwaffe continued to mount bombing raids against British towns and cities in the "Blitz." Daylight raids were abandoned in favor of nighttime attacks. As well as continuing raids against London, German bombers struck other cities, including Coventry, Birmingham, Sheffield, Liverpool, and Manchester. But it was London that was hit the hardest. On the night of December 29–30, 1940, 130 bombers bombed the city,

engulfing an area between St. Paul's Cathedral and the Guildhall. The Blitz continued into 1941, often inflicting heavy casualties. On May 10–11, for example, more than 1,400 civilians were killed by bombs. But British morale did not crack in the face of Nazi aggression. The Blitz continued until the Germans invaded the Soviet Union in June 1941.

◀ **A bomb crater in front of the Royal Exchange, Threadneedle Street, London, January 1941. The bomb struck the booking hall of Bank Underground station, the blast traveling through the tunnels and killing 111 people who had taken shelter there. The Bank of England is on the left in the image.**

▼ **The Royal Exchange in London was formerly a financial exchange. Built in the sixteenth century, it was opened by Queen Elizabeth I in 1571. The exchange was closed in 1939. It is now filled with shops and restaurants.**

▶ On May 10, 1941, St. Pancras railway station was hit by a German bomb that smashed through the roof and exploded between platforms 3 and 4. The explosion was absorbed mostly by the rolling stock, thus saving the structural integrity of the station.

▶ St. Pancras underwent an extensive redevelopment in the early 2000s to restore it to its Victorian glory. It is used by 45 million passengers annually and is one of the largest railway stations in Britain.

◀ Bomb damage in Regent Street, October 1940, the month the Luftwaffe abandoned daylight bombing due to heavy aircraft losses. London was hit by 400 parachute mines and 28,000 high-explosive bombs over the next eight months.

◀ Purpose-built as a shopping street and opened in 1819, Regent Street still contains its iconic nineteenth-century facades and remains a center for exclusive shopping and high-end brands.

CRETE
MAY 1941

On May 20, 1941, 10,000 German paratroopers dropped on the British-occupied island of Crete in a daring airborne operation. Success would hinge on the capture of key airfields at Maleme, Retimo, and Heraklion. The island garrison of 27,500 British troops and 14,000 Greeks put up a heroic fight but had been evicted from the island by May 27. The battle was a savage one: one in four paratroopers dropped on Crete were killed, with many more wounded. Hitler was so shocked at the losses incurred on Crete that he canceled an airborne assault on the island of Malta that was planned for 1942.

◀ A German Ju 52 transport aircraft in flames over Maleme airfield on May 20. Each Ju 52 could carry sixteen fully equipped paratroopers; 500 of them were used during the drops on Crete. It took days of fighting to capture Maleme.

▲ The German war cemetery near Maleme airport on the north coast of Crete contains the graves of 4,465 soldiers who died on the island during World War II, most of them paratroopers who were dropped in May 1941.

MOSCOW
RUSSIA, NOVEMBER 1941

The Germans invaded the Soviet Union in June 1941. After a series of spectacular victories, in the fall the German Army was poised to launch an assault on the Soviet capital. To take Moscow, the Germans amassed 1.9 million troops and 1,000 tanks against 1.25 million Red Army troops and 990 tanks. The assault, code-named Operation Typhoon, began on October 2 and initially swept all before it. But then fall rains reduced roads to mud and slowed the advance. The arrival of subzero temperatures hardened the ground, and the panzers were able to advance; by November 22, the lead

units of the German Army were only 30 miles north of Moscow. However, the German units were under half strength and exhausted, and many vehicles were immobilized due to a lack of fuel. Typhoon ground to a halt on December 5. The next day the Red Army launched a devastating counterattack that saved Moscow.

◀ **A parade in Moscow's Red Square on November 7, 1941, to commemorate the twenty-fourth anniversary of the October Revolution. Snow and thick clouds prevented German aircraft from bombing Moscow that day, giving a huge boost to Russian morale.**

▼ **Moscow's Red Square today. The huge square has always held a special place in the Russian psyche. For nearly 600 years it has been the site of Russian leaders displaying their military might. The striking Saint Basil's Cathedral can be seen in the background.**

DEFENSE OF MOSCOW The Soviet authorities mobilized the city's population to build strongpoints to halt the Germans, some 600,000 Muscovites over the age of eighteen being conscripted. They worked with spades and picks to dig anti-tank ditches and trenches. There was a defensive line outside the city that ran from the Moscow–Volga Canal in the north to Serpukhov in the south. Inside Moscow, there were three lines of defense: one along the Circular Railway Ring, one along the Garden Ring, and one along the Boulevard Ring, the last line of defense before Red Square and the Kremlin.

◀ **Top: Anti-aircraft gunners on the roof of the 1,000-room Moskva Hotel, built in a corner of Red Square in 1930 and since demolished. The anti-aircraft guns are four Maxim M1910 heavy machine guns. Bottom: The Red Square skyline today. In the distance stands Triumph Palace, a residential building erected at the start of the twenty-first century.**

▶ **Top: A sandbag barricade at the intersection of Balchug Street and Lubochny Lane, built to defend the Kremlin during the Battle of Moscow. This was part of the last line of Soviet defense as Lubochny Lane is near Red Square. Bottom: Today, Lubochny Lane is the second-shortest street in Moscow. It connects two bridges over the Moskva River: the Chugunny and the Bolshoy Moskvoretsky.**

PEARL HARBOR

HAWAII, DECEMBER 7, 1941

In attacking Pearl Harbor, Hawaii, the Japanese planned to cripple the U.S. Pacific Fleet, to allow their conquest of the Philippines, Malaya, Burma, and the Dutch East Indies before America could respond. The surprise attack by carrier-borne aircraft sank five battleships and three destroyers, damaged three battleships and two cruisers, and killed or wounded 3,478 military personnel. Described by President Franklin D. Roosevelt as a "day which will live in infamy," the brilliant tactical success stirred an enraged United States to enter the conflict.

◀ Struck by Japanese bombs, some of which hit its forward magazines, causing catastrophic damage, the battleship USS *Arizona* burns furiously in Pearl Harbor. More than 1,100 of its crew were killed.

▼ Opened in 1962, the Pearl Harbor National Memorial spans the middle section of the sunken USS *Arizona* and is visited by more than a million people a year. The American flag flies from a flagpole attached to the severed mainmast of the battleship.

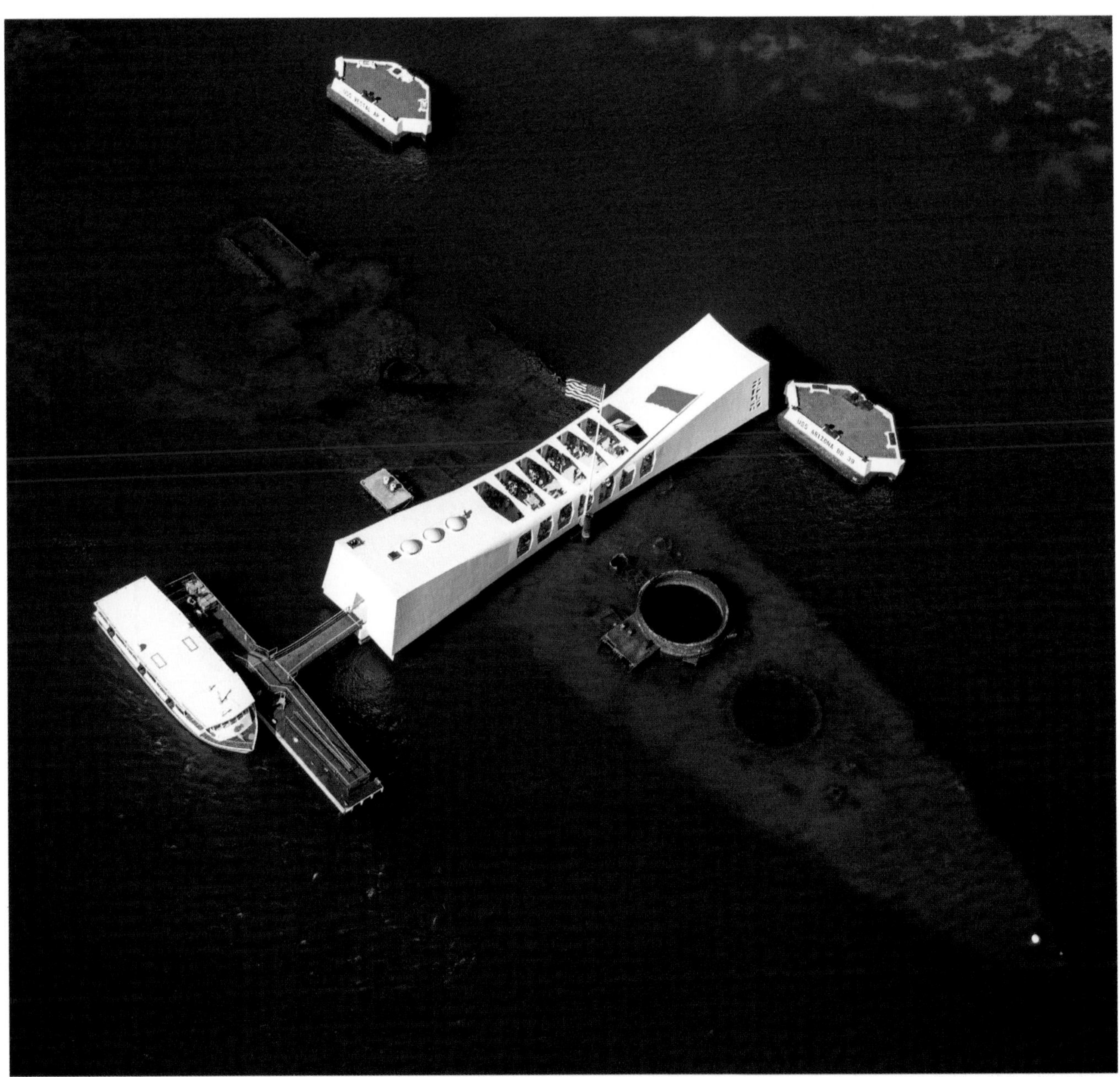

PEARL HARBOR NAVAL STATION Located eight miles west of Honolulu on the island of Oahu, Pearl Harbor has been a U.S. naval base since 1908, when it was called the Pearl Harbor Naval Station. It did not become a major strategic asset to the U.S. Navy immediately, however. Indeed, the Pacific Fleet was only ordered to leave San Diego and transfer to Pearl Harbor in 1940, in response to the growing Japanese threat.

◀ **An aerial view of Pearl Harbor, looking southwest, on October 30, 1940. Ford Island Naval Air Station is at center. Just beyond it, across the channel, is the Pearl Harbor Navy Yard. The airfield at top center of the picture is the U.S. Army's Hickam Field. Japanese pilots would have had such a bird's-eye view when they flew in on December 7, 1941.**

▲ **A photograph taken from a Japanese aircraft showing "battleship row" on the far side of Ford Island being attacked. A torpedo has just hit the USS *West Virginia*. The USS *Arizona* sits second from the left and has yet to be struck.**

▶ **Today, Pearl Harbor remains an active military base. It is the home of the U.S. Pacific Fleet and is the navy's busiest port. Its facilities include a shipyard, a supply center, and a submarine base.**

DIEPPE
FRANCE, AUGUST 1942

The Dieppe raid involved 200 vessels, 6,000 troops, and 3,000 naval personnel. It was launched to test the Allied amphibious landing capability against entrenched German shore defenses, as a precursor to an invasion of Hitler's "Fortress Europe." It failed in every regard. The first British amphibious landing since the Gallipoli campaign in 1915, losses totaled nearly 4,000 men killed or captured. However, increased German confidence following their successful defense of Dieppe led them to believe any future Allied landings would be directed against ports. They therefore concentrated on reinforcing defenses around ports to the detriment of beaches. On D-Day, the Allies would land on beaches.

▲ **Knocked-out tanks and abandoned landing craft on one of Dieppe's beaches after the raid. There were few less-suited locations on the French coast for an amphibious landing. The deep beach shale, for example, was unsuitable for tanks, many of which got stuck.**

▲ Today, the cliffs overlooking the beaches are unchanged. Allied intelligence failed to identify cavelike enemy gun positions in the cliffs before the landings.

► A German cliff-top machine-gun position at Dieppe. The Germans began actively preparing defenses in the Dieppe area in March 1942. This tripod-mounted MG 34 had a range of 11,655 feet and could fire 900 rounds a minute. Such weapons were lethal against soldiers coming ashore on beaches.

EL ALAMEIN

NORTH AFRICA, OCTOBER 1942

In the summer of 1942, the British 8th Army had been pushed back to the Egyptian village of El Alamein by Erwin Rommel's Panzer Army Africa. Fortunately for the British, the Germans were in no shape to advance further, allowing the commander of the 8th Army, General Bernard Montgomery, to receive reinforcements. When he launched the Battle of El Alamein on October 23, 1942, his army possessed more than 1,000 tanks to Rommel's 490, which included 278 obsolete Italian models. Rommel was also outnumbered in the air. Maintaining incessant air and ground attack, Montgomery's forces smashed through enemy lines. El Alamein signaled the eventual defeat of Axis forces in North Africa.

◀◀ At El Alamein, the 8th Army received new equipment, such as American Sherman tanks and these British Churchill tanks. The Churchill had thick armor and strong firepower. Note the dust kicked up by the tanks.

◀ Many armored vehicles knocked out during the Battle of El Alamein were abandoned in the desert. They are still there today, including this Axis armored car, the dry conditions preserving their hulls for posterity.

STALINGRAD

RUSSIA, JULY 1942–FEBRUARY 1943

The Battle of Stalingrad was one of the pivotal moments of World War II. The German summer offensive of 1942 became bogged down in the city of Stalingrad in the fall. The city was bombed heavily by the Luftwaffe before ground troops went in, the fighting degenerating into a vicious close-quarters battle in the city ruins. The fighting raged to and fro for weeks, the Red Army feeding in troops across the Volga River to prevent the Germans from capturing the city. The Soviets launched a counterattack to the west of Stalingrad in November, which surrounded German troops in the city. The survivors surrendered on February 2, 1943.

◀ This photograph was taken in August 1942, following a massive Luftwaffe air raid. It shows a fountain of a statue of six children dancing around a crocodile. It was called the Barmaley Fountain after a Russian fairy tale in which a young boy named Barmaley is eaten by a giant crocodile.

▶ Though restored after the war, the original fountain was destroyed in the 1950s. A replica has since been built and has stood in the same square in front of the railway station since 2013.

PAVLOV'S HOUSE In the house-to-house fighting that raged in Stalingrad in the fall of 1942, the battle for Pavlov's House became one of the most famous episodes. Some 300 yards from the Volga River, the four-story building was occupied by a platoon from the Red Army's 42nd Guards Regiment. When the platoon commander, Lieutenant Afanasyev, was blinded in the fighting, Sergeant Yakov Pavlov took over command. He and his men defended the building for 58 days in the face of ferocious German attacks.

▲ **Above left: Pavlov's House, ca. 1942. The men knocked holes in the walls on the top floor to use anti-tank rifles against German panzers. Above right: Soldiers sheltering in a trench during the battle, with Pavlov's House visible in the background.**

◀ **Pavlov's House was the first building in Stalingrad to be restored after the war. In 1985, a memorial wall was erected on one of its sides.**

MAMAYEV KURGAN A hill in the center of the city, Mamayev Kurgan had a commanding position over the whole area, including the Volga River. In the battle for control of Stalingrad, both sides realized that whoever held Mamayev Kurgan would hold the city. As such, it became the center of fierce fighting for weeks.

▲ **After the battle, Mamayev Kurgan was littered with bodies, unexploded ordnance, and wrecked military equipment. For years afterward, no grass grew on its slopes. Bullets and fragments of bone can still be found on the hill.**

► **The 300-foot-tall statue *The Motherland Calls* dominates the Mamayev Kurgan today and is but one memorial to those who fell at Stalingrad (now Volgograd). The hill is the grave of 34,000 soldiers killed at Stalingrad.**

KURSK
RUSSIA, JULY 1943

Aside from the Pripet Marshes, European Russia is filled with relatively flat, wide-open spaces that are ideal for armored warfare. The German panzers made huge gains as they advanced east in 1941, during Operation Barbarossa. Two years later, following the disaster at Stalingrad, Hitler launched another offensive to regain the initiative on the Eastern Front. Code-named Citadel, it involved 700,000 troops and 2,500 tanks and assault guns tasked with destroying Red Army forces in the Kursk salient, which was filled

with soldiers, tanks, artillery, and field works. The battle was fought over a huge area of rolling, open terrain, most of which has remained unchanged since July 1943. The Germans launched their attack on July 5, but had been beaten by July 13. The open terrain meant there was no cover for either tanks or infantry, and losses were high, the Red Army suffering more than 177,000 casualties. German losses were 50,000 casualties. The battlefield was filled with burning tanks.

◄ **German Panzer IV tanks during the early phase of Kursk. The terrain is typical of the battlefield, though judging by the undisturbed ground and open hatches, the fighting is some way off.**

▲ **The decisive clash at Kursk was fought at Prokhorovka on July 12, 1943. There is now a memorial complex on the spot to honor the Russian dead, including a belfry surmounted by a figure of the Virgin Mary. Note how flat the surrounding terrain is.**

SALERNO

ITALY, SEPTEMBER 1943

The Allies chose Salerno, southeast of Naples, as the target for their invasion of mainland Italy. Operation Avalanche was mounted by 165,000 Allied troops of Lieutenant General Mark Clark's U.S. 5th Army. The Salerno landings began on September 9, and Allied units drove inland. The Germans counterattacked on September 13, driving back the Allies and threatening the entire bridgehead. In echoes of Dunkirk, Clark considered ordering an evacuation, but massive Allied naval bombardments and aerial attacks forced the Germans back. On September 19, Clark's units began the advance on Naples and by the end of the month all southern Italy was under Allied control.

◀ The port of Salerno, about 50 miles south of Naples, was crucial for receiving supplies after the invasion beaches had been secured. The port was captured by British commandos on September 10. They then advanced to Naples, though only after nine days of heavy fighting.

▼ Salerno pictured today. Now, as then, it has excellent sea approaches, which is partly why the Allies chose it as a landing site. At the time, the beaches also had light defenses.

▶ Right: Troops of the U.S. 408th Battalion, 36th Infantry Division, in the ruins of the Temple of Hera in the ancient town of Paestum, September 1943. There was intense fighting in and around the town for nine days before the Germans withdrew to the north. Far right: Today, the ruins remain exactly as they were in 1943.

DOMINVS DEVS SABAOTH

ORTONA
ITALY, DECEMBER 1943

Referred to as the "Stalingrad of Italy," the battle for the Adriatic town of Ortona was fought between the Canadian 1st Infantry Division and the elite German 1st Parachute Division. The fighting began on December 20, Canadian tanks and infantry suffering heavy losses in the town's narrow streets. The Germans booby-trapped buildings and rubble, and snipers made the streets killing zones. So, the Canadian troops fought house to house, blasting holes in walls to allow them to advance. Ortona was cleared by December 28, by which time the Canadians had suffered 2,300 casualties, including 500 killed.

◀ **Built on the site of a Roman temple, the Basilica of St. Thomas the Apostle was severely damaged during the fighting in Ortona. A favored tactic of the Germans was to pack basements with explosives, which they then detonated remotely.**

▶ **The cathedral, like many damaged churches and cathedrals throughout Italy, was restored at great cost in the 1950s and 1960s.**

CASSINO

ITALY, JANUARY 1944

At the beginning of 1944, the Allies were ready to launch their offensive against the German Gustav Line, link up with units landed by sea further up the coast at Anzio, and then capture Rome. But the Germans had fortified the heights that dominated this part of central Italy, nowhere more so than the monastery on Monte Cassino. The initial Allied attack, launched on January 17, was repulsed with heavy casualties. Thus began five months of desperate fighting around the monastery, which was defended by German paratroopers. It was only when the Allies had broken through the Gustav Line elsewhere in mid-May that the Germans withdrew from Monte Cassino.

◄ **Top: The Allies initially spared the monastery from air attack, but sightings of German troops within its walls changed their minds. They proceeded to unleash some 230 bombers against the monastery.**

◄ **The bombers made their strike on February 15. Much of the building was destroyed, though the subterranean chambers in which the defenders took cover were not damaged. An Allied assault later that day was defeated with heavy losses.**

▲ **The restoration of the monastery at Monte Cassino was paid for by the Italian government. Work lasted a decade from the late 1940s to the end of the 1950s. It was reconsecrated by Pope Paul VI in 1964.**

NORMANDY
FRANCE, JUNE 6, 1944

Operation Overlord, the Allied invasion of France, was the greatest amphibious operation in history. In the initial assault, 50,000 men landed on five beaches in Normandy. American troops landed on Utah and Omaha Beaches, the British landed on Gold and Sword Beaches, and the Canadians landed on Juno Beach. In addition, three Allied airborne divisions were dropped behind the beaches. Despite heavy losses on Omaha Beach, by the end of June 6, Allied soldiers had a toehold in Nazi-occupied Europe and were there to stay. The 11,000 aircraft the Allies deployed ensured aerial superiority over the beaches and Normandy hinterland. The gamble had paid off.

◀ Canadian troops come ashore at Bernières-sur-Mer on Juno Beach. Once ashore, the Canadians were tasked with seizing the Caen–Bayeux road and high ground west of Caen.

▼ Juno Beach today. The timber-framed building is "Canada House," one of the first houses liberated by Canadian soldiers. The stone structure next to the house is a memorial to the soldiers, sailors, and airmen who fought on Juno Beach that day.

SAINT-LÔ

FRANCE, JULY 1944

Key to the battle for Normandy, being an intersection of major roads, the town of Saint-Lô was targeted by Allied bombers and artillery. The bocage-type landscape, typically filled with hedgerows, made the fight for the town bloody and time-consuming. Between July 3 and 22, more than 11,000 GIs were killed in the battle and its immediate aftermath. When American soldiers entered the town on July 18, they found mostly rubble. Around 95 percent of its buildings had been destroyed in the fighting.

◀ In the aftermath of the fight for the town, Saint-Lô was nicknamed "the Capital of Ruins." Ironically, much of the damage inflicted on the town was the result of a raid by Allied bombers on June 6, with instructions to flatten Saint-Lô.

▼ The Church of Notre-Dame was heavily damaged during the air raid in June 1944. Restored after the war, the front of the church was left as it appeared after the fighting in July 1944.

FALAISE
FRANCE, AUGUST 1944

Following the capture of Saint-Lô, General Patton's U.S. 3rd Army raced east and then turned north, cutting off German forces fighting the British and Canadians there. The Germans in Normandy were now in danger of being surrounded in a pocket west of the towns of Argentan and Falaise. If the Allies could close the pocket, they would destroy the German Army in France. In desperation, the Germans began to retreat east, holding a 10-mile exit from the pocket for five days, all the time being attacked from the air and assaulted by ground units (Allied aircraft were flying up to 3,000

sorties a day against those trapped in the pocket). On August 19, the Allied pincers snapped shut and three days later the Falaise Pocket was eliminated. The battle cost the Germans 10,000 dead and 50,000 prisoners; 350 tanks and 1,000 artillery pieces were destroyed. The Germans were now in headlong retreat from France.

◀ **Thousands of German prisoners in the Nonant-le-Pin prisoner-of-war camp after their surrender in the Falaise Pocket. Exhausted and hungry, they were glad to be out of the fighting (very few attempted to escape during the camp's existence).**

▼ **The site of the Nonant-le-Pin prisoner-of-war camp today, where no traces remain. Being in the camp had kept German prisoners safe from vengeful French citizens and execution by the French Resistance.**

SIEGFRIED LINE

GERMANY, SEPTEMBER 1944

Known to the Allies as the Siegfried Line, Germany's West Wall was a defensive system on its western border. Work started in 1936, and by 1938 some 500,000 men were building the wall, using a third of Germany's annual cement production. Eventually, the wall ran from Holland in the north to Switzerland in the south, a 400-mile chain of more than 3,000 concrete pillboxes, bunkers, and observation posts. Work halted in 1940, following Germany's victory over France. In the fall of 1944, with Allied armies approaching, the West Wall was deficient in mines, barbed wire, artillery, and anti-tank weapons. Nevertheless the Germans put up a stout defense and Allied troops spent three months fighting to breach it.

◀ March 1945. With the war in Europe nearly over, British prime minister Winston Churchill visited the Siegfried Line. With him are, left to right, Field Marshal Bernard Montgomery, Field Marshal Sir Alan Brooke, and General William Simpson.

▼ The most distinctive feature of the West Wall were the "dragon's teeth," concrete anti-tank obstacles arranged in five rows. As a result of their durable construction and the number that were built, western Germany is still filled with thousands of them, plans to remove them having proved too costly.

◀ Two American soldiers look down on dragon's teeth in the Siegfried Line. The Allies incurred heavy casualties in the three months spent trying to breach the defense.

ARNHEM

NETHERLANDS, SEPTEMBER 1944

In September 1944, the Allies launched Operation Market Garden, which involved dropping three airborne divisions behind enemy lines to seize key bridges to allow a rapid drive into Germany. The target of the British 1st Airborne was the bridge over the Neder Rijn River at Arnhem, the northernmost objective. The drop took place on September 17, men of the 2nd Parachute Battalion reaching the northern side of the road bridge. Attempts to reach the southern side were beaten back, the battalion was soon surrounded by SS soldiers, and a desperate battle began in Arnhem. With no hope of relief and short of ammunition and food, the 2nd Parachute Battalion surrendered on September 21.

◀ After fighting in Arnhem had ended, the Germans ordered the evacuation of the city, which became a military zone. Empty homes were then looted of anything of value, plunder being sent back to bombed-out civilians in Germany.

▼ Modern Arnhem with the road bridge in the background. Such was the damage inflicted upon the city that it took until 1969 before Arnhem was fully restored, the Germans having destroyed many homes after the surrender of the 2nd Parachute Battalion.

ARDENNES

LUXEMBOURG AND BELGIUM, DECEMBER 1944

The German offensive code-named Watch on the Rhine involved 500,000 troops and 1,500 tanks. Its objective was to sweep through the Ardennes, capture Antwerp, and destroy Allied armies in Belgium and Holland. In fog, rain, and snow, the offensive began on December 16, 1944, and was initially successful. But progress was slow along forest roads, and the advance was held up by American troops defending the town

of Bastogne. The German armies formed a bulge into Allied territory, but progressed no further. Attempts to take Bastogne failed and the weather began to clear, allowing Allied aircraft to attack German units. Allied ground units pushed the Germans back in early January 1945, and by January 16, Hitler's divisions were at their start positions again, with 120,000 dead, wounded, and missing. Watch on the Rhine had failed.

◀ **On December 16, the town of Clervaux, Luxembourg, was attacked by the Germans. Soldiers of the U.S. 110th Infantry Regiment put up a heroic resistance against the tanks of the 2nd Panzer Division, retreating into the castle to continue fighting. They surrendered on December 18.**

▲ **During the fighting in Clervaux, German tank rounds and grenades started a fire in the castle that destroyed large parts of the building. The castle has since been restored to its former glory.**

IWO JIMA
JAPAN, FEBRUARY 1945

The island of Iwo Jima lay only 760 miles from Tokyo and its capture would provide a base for U.S. aircraft bombing Japan. Three U.S. Marine Divisions (70,000 men) were tasked with capturing the island, defended by 20,000 Japanese in a warren of pillboxes and strongpoints. The invasion began on February 9. Of the 20,000 Marines that landed, 2,500 were killed or wounded, marking the start of an intense, bloody battle that would continue until March 25. By this time, 6,000 Americans were dead and 17,000 wounded. Of the Japanese garrison, only 216 survived to become prisoners of war. The island was soon operating as an American air base.

▼ **Damaged American amphibious tractors and boats lie on the beach at Iwo Jima. Each tractor could carry up to thirty fully armed soldiers, who rolled over the sides to disembark.**

◀ In one of the most iconic images from World War II, taken by Marine Corps combat photographer Sergeant Lou Lowery, men of the 28th Marine Regiment raise the Stars and Stripes above Mount Suribachi on February 23. Only three of the Marines photographed survived the fighting on Iwo Jima, which would continue for another month.

▼ The black volcanic sand is a distinctive feature of the beaches on Iwo Jima, as are the steep sand embankments. In the distance is Mount Suribachi, which was heavily fortified by the Japanese in 1945.

REICHSWALD

GERMANY, FEBRUARY 1945

Operation Veritable, launched on February 8, also called the Battle of the Reichswald, was designed to clear German forces from the area between the Meuse and Rhine Rivers. The Canadian 1st Army and a British corps attacked from the north, the American 9th Army from the south. The fighting in the forest was vicious, the Allies battling enemy

troops in entrenchments and behind barbed wire. General Dwight D. Eisenhower described the Battle of the Reichswald as "one of the fiercest and most violent campaigns of the war, a bitter struggle for endurance between the Allies and the Germans." When the fighting ended on March 11, 60,000 men had been killed or wounded in the Reichswald.

◀ **British infantry hitch a lift on tanks during the Battle of the Reichswald. There were only two major roads on which the Allies could advance through the forest. The terrain was a defender's dream: valleys and hills, thick woods, and narrow trails.**

▲ **The Reichswald Forest is still filled with trenches, dugouts, and mortar pits from the fighting in February 1945.**

SEELOW HEIGHTS

GERMANY, APRIL 1945

The Seelow Heights, to the east of Berlin, were the scene of vicious fighting at the start of the Soviet Red Army's Berlin offensive. The heights were defended by 112,000 Germans, their commander, General Heinrici, opening the dams farther up the Oder River to turn the ground between the river and the heights into a swamp. On April 16, the first Red Army attack was thrown back, but further assaults on April 17 and 18 broke through the German lines. On April 19, the Red Army smashed through the Seelow Heights at a cost of 30,000 dead. The road to the west and Berlin was open.

◀ Red Army artillery fire at German positions on the Seelow Heights in April 1945. For the offensive to take Berlin, the Red Army amassed 41,000 artillery pieces. This allowed Red Army commanders to deploy 260 artillery pieces on each half mile of front to support the advance. To defeat such firepower, German troops would often withdraw before bombardments so Russian shells "punched air."

▼ Thousands of Russian and German men fell during the battle for the Seelow Heights. Many bodies still lie in the ground and efforts are underway to retrieve them. Nineteen digs across less than half a square mile uncovered the remains of 116 German and 129 Russian soldiers. The area is also still littered with grenades and artillery shells.

BERLIN

GERMANY, APRIL–MAY 1945

The Berlin offensive began on April 16, 1945, and by April 20, Red Army artillery was shelling the city's eastern suburbs. In the skies, more than 7,000 Russian aircraft were bombing and strafing German troops and positions. The defenders simply did not have the men or ammunition to withstand the Soviet onslaught. By April 24, there was fighting throughout the city, and by April 28, Russian troops were one mile from Hitler's bunker below the Chancellery. The bitter street fighting was

costly for both sides, the battle for the Reichstag killing half of its 5,000 defenders. The shot-pummeled building fell on May 1 (Hitler and his wife Eva Braun had committed suicide the day before). Berlin fell on May 2, by which time 500,000 Germans had been killed or captured and the Red Army had suffered 81,000 killed and 272,000 wounded. The Third Reich had fallen.

◀ **The Soviet flag is raised in May 1945. This shot was taken by the Soviet war reporter Yevgeny Khaldei and is a reconstruction of the event that took place on the night of April 30. The Red Army soldiers in the picture are Meliton Kantaria (holding the flag) and Abdulkhakim Ismailov.**

▲ **The same view from the modern Reichstag. Inside, the rebuilt building retains some of the bomb damage and communist graffiti scrawled on the walls by victorious Red Army soldiers in May 1945.**

REICHSTAG Commissioned by Chancellor Otto von Bismarck twenty years after German unification in 1871, to celebrate the founding of the Second Reich, the Reichstag (parliament) was the seat of government in the German Empire and the Weimar Republic. Gutted by fire in 1933, during World War II, the building was bombed, and in 1945 it was blasted by Red Army artillery. Partly refurbished in the 1960s, after German reunification the decision was taken to move the seat of government back to the Reichstag. The building was fully renovated by the architect Sir Norman Foster and reopened in 1999.

◀◀ Crew members of a Red Army tank survey the ruins of the Reichstag in May 1945. The structure was one of more than 600,000 buildings destroyed in Berlin during the war.

◀ The Bundesrat represents the sixteen states of Germany at the federal level. It meets at the former Prussian House of Lords in Berlin, seen here. The Bundestag, the federal parliament, meets in the Reichstag.

◀ The ruins of the Reichstag following the German surrender in May 1945. The building had been the target of Russian tanks and artillery before the Red Army infantry attacked. Ironically, construction costs had been financed by French reparations after the 1870 Franco–Prussian War.

▼ The new Reichstag features a transparent glass and steel dome, open to the public. As well as housing the German parliament, the building has become one of the country's top tourist attractions.

TIERGARTEN Berlin's Tiergarten is a large, forested park close to the government district. Originally a seventeenth-century royal hunting park, it was badly damaged during the battle for the city in 1945. A huge flak tower—a massive concrete structure—located in the park took part in the battle for the Reichstag, lowering its anti-aircraft guns to shoot at Red Army targets. The tower was attacked by the 79th Guards Rifle Division, but they could make no impression on the building. Its defenders were eventually allowed to surrender.

▼ **After the fighting in Berlin had ended, Tiergarten was strewn with water-filled shell craters. The trees would soon disappear, as they were cut down by freezing Berliners to provide fuel in the absence of coal supplies.**

▶ **The same view today, looking east along Strasse des 17. Juni toward the city. From 1949, Tiergarten was replanted with trees supplied from other parts of Germany.**

COLOGNE

GERMANY, SEPTEMBER 1945

A large city, Cologne possesses one of the key inland ports in Europe. It is also the economic capital of the Rhineland and one of the busiest rail junctions in Germany. All these things meant the city was a major target for Allied bombers and armies in World War II. The city was the target of 262 air raids during the war, the largest of which, the 1,000-bomber raid of May 1942, created a firestorm that destroyed the center of the city. Only the cathedral was left standing and 100,000 people were made homeless. Many

fled the city, and by March 1945, out of a prewar population of 770,000, only 20,000 residents remained. The American 3rd Armored Division entered the devastated city on March 6, 1945, much fighting taking place around the cathedral before the German defenders were defeated (a German Panther tank was knocked out in front of the cathedral).

◀ **Cologne Cathedral behind the damaged Hohenzollern Bridge spanning the Rhine. Hugely important to the Germans during the war, the three-arched structure had four railway tracks and a roadway. The Germans destroyed it in March 1945 to prevent its use by the Allies.**

▲ **Repair work began on the Hohenzollern Bridge after the war. By 1948, pedestrians were able to cross, but it was not until 1959 that trains were again using the bridge. Today it is one of the busiest bridges in Germany, some 1,200 trains crossing daily.**

2,000-YEAR-OLD CITY Cologne was awarded a city charter in AD 50 as part of the Roman Empire. Strategically located on the banks of the Rhine, it developed into Germany's wealthiest city in medieval times. Briefly under the control of revolutionary France, it was awarded to Prussia in 1815. The French had demolished many of the churches during their reign, providing space for factories to be built inside the city during the Industrial Revolution, which then sparked a rapid increase in Cologne's population. By the twentieth century, the city was a major industrial center, leading to the heavy bombing during World War II.

◀ **The cathedral and damaged Hohenzollern Bridge in 1945. Ironically, the structure was the only bridge in Cologne not to be destroyed by Allied bombers in World War II. The large ornamental gates at each end of the bridge were not rebuilt.**

▼ **Even today, tons of unexploded ordnance from Allied air raids are unearthed in Cologne each year. In the rush to reconstruct Germany, many bombs were buried in rubble or encased in concrete, only to be discovered during the construction of new buildings.**

ORDENSBURG VOGELSANG

GERMANY, SEPTEMBER 1945

A year after they came to power in 1933, the Nazis began building "Order Castles"—Ordensburgen—to train future leaders of the Third Reich. Three were built, one being the Ordensburg in Vogelsang in the Eifel, Westphalia. Built on a hillside overlooking Lake Urft, the Vogelsang complex opened in 1936 and cadets began receiving instruction in the same year. However, the outbreak of war in 1939 interrupted the project and a 2,000-bed extension was never built. During the war the site housed German citizens from bombed cities. It was occupied by the Americans in February 1945 and subsequently turned over to the British.

◄ **The work of architect Clemens Klotz, the design for Vogelsang was based on that of a medieval castle. The water tower was supposed to represent a castle keep. One of the tests undertaken by students was combat with bare hands against wild dogs.**

▲ **The Ordensburg Vogelsang has been open to the public since 2006 and is also used as a conference venue. The surrounding woods contain nature trails.**

OKINAWA
JAPAN, APRIL–JUNE 1945

The Americans invaded Okinawa, one of the Japanese home islands, on April 1, 1945, to provide a logistical base for the proposed U.S. invasion of Japan. Against a garrison of more than 100,000 soldiers and home guard, the Americans committed as many as 180,000 soldiers, Marines, and naval personnel. The fanatical Japanese resistance slowed the

advance and caused heavy casualties. Nevertheless, by the end of April, the castle of Shuri, the linchpin of the Japanese defenses in the south of the island, had been captured. Fighting on the island ended on June 22, with more than 110,000 Japanese soldiers and civilians having been killed. American casualties stood at 39,420.

◀ **A U.S. Marine Corps Grasshopper observation aircraft flying over the ruins of the Okinawan capital of Naha, on the southern coast of the island. The city was pounded by naval gunfire and air raids, reducing much of Naha to rubble.**

▼ **After the war, Naha was rebuilt, the American military taking over the port and instigating extensive renovations of the deep-water facility. Many Japanese earned money salvaging sunken American ships near the coast.**

HIROSHIMA
JAPAN, AUGUST 1945

American planners believed an invasion of Japan would cost an estimated one million casualties. Such losses being unacceptable, the decision was made to demand the unconditional surrender of the Japanese. To reject this would result in Japan being subjected to—in President Harry S. Truman's words—a "rain of ruin from the air, the like of which has never been seen on Earth." Tokyo rejected the ultimatum, so the decision was taken to drop an atomic bomb on the city of Hiroshima. The city was chosen because it had not been

bombed to date and scientists could study the effects of an atomic blast more easily. On August 6, 1945, the B-29 *Enola Gay* dropped the bomb "Little Boy" on Hiroshima. The resulting mushroom cloud could be seen hundreds of miles away. On the ground, 40,000 people died instantly, 20,000 more would die from wounds and radiation poisoning, and 60,000 others were injured to varying degrees.

◀ **Because the atomic bomb was detonated above the city, the blast was directed vertically, which meant the walls of the city's Industrial Promotion Hall were left standing. Everything else around it was destroyed. The building became known as the Atomic Bomb Dome.**

▲ **In 1996, the building became a UN World Cultural Heritage Site and now serves as the Hiroshima Peace Memorial. It is surrounded by the Peace Memorial Park. The dome itself has undergone three conservation projects since 1967.**

NAGASAKI
JAPAN, AUGUST 1945

Despite the devastation inflicted on Hiroshima, the Japanese government still refused to surrender. The Americans could have starved Japan into surrender and continued their bombing campaign, but Washington wanted to speed up the end of the war. Therefore, President Truman ordered a second atomic bomb to be dropped on a Japanese city. At 11:00 a.m. on August 9, the B-29 Superfortress *Bockscar* dropped "Fat Man" on the city of

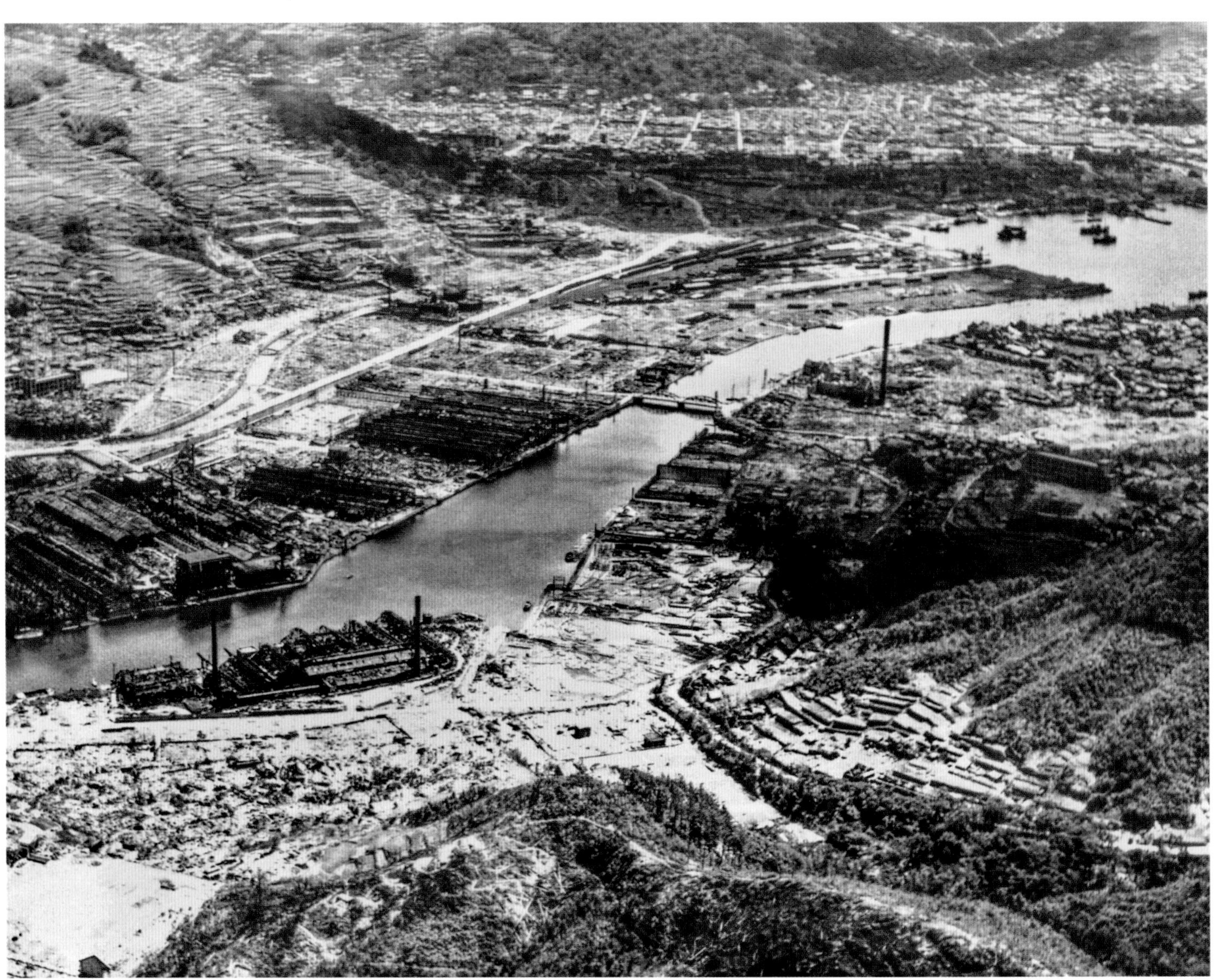

Nagasaki. The plutonium bomb did not reap as deadly a toll as "Little Boy," but it still killed 36,000 instantly and injured 60,000 more, the majority civilians. Thousands more people would die from radiation poisoning in the months that followed. At 12:00 p.m. on August 15, 1945, Emperor Hirohito broadcast a cease-fire announcement on the radio.

◀ **Nagasaki lies in a natural bowl, which helped trap some of the atomic bomb's destructive effect. The city of 286,000 people was totally destroyed by the blast, the wooden houses vaporizing instantly.**

▲ **The reconstruction of Nagasaki began in 1946 and the city is once more a thriving port. There are shrines to those killed in the bomb blast all over the city. Many of the survivors of August 9, 1945, called *hibakusha*, have now sadly passed away.**

1950—1953
KOREAN WAR

INCHON

SOUTH KOREA, SEPTEMBER 1950

In June 1950, North Korean troops launched an invasion of South Korea. By the end of July, South Korean forces and their U.S. allies had been forced back to Pusan in the southeast of the country. To relieve the pressure, General Douglas MacArthur, commander of UN forces in Korea, mounted a daring amphibious assault on Inchon, deep behind North Korean lines. The 1st Marine Division landed at Inchon on September 15, and by the next day had secured it. Using the port as a springboard, U.S. and South Korean forces struck east to Seoul, capturing it on September 27. The North Koreans had been overwhelmed by the Inchon landings.

◄ The Marines landed on three beaches at Inchon. This is the scene on Red Beach on September 15, after the fighting had moved inland. Vehicles and supplies are being offloaded from the ships.

► The beaches at Inchon have a slight gradient, making them ideal for amphibious landings. However, offshore, the sea contains many treacherous silt banks, all of which had to be negotiated by landing craft.

SEOUL
SOUTH KOREA, SEPTEMBER 1950

Following the Inchon landings, U.S. Marines and South Korean forces advanced east toward Seoul, the occupied South Korean capital. Supported by aircraft dropping bombs and napalm, the Americans took Gimpo airfield outside the city on September 18, North Korean forces suffering heavy casualties as they fell back into the city. Seoul's garrison numbered 20,000 men, so taking the Han River and the ridge overlooking the city was hard and entailed heavy losses. Nevertheless, by the evening of September 15, UN forces had

Seoul surrounded. Supported by air strikes, UN forces entered the city and fought block by block against entrenched North Korean soldiers. The city was demolished in the fighting as tanks and aircraft pummeled North Korean positions. On September 27, as fighting raged around it, UN forces captured the American consulate and raised the American flag over the building. The battles at Inchon and Seoul resulted in the capture of 125,000 North Korean soldiers and the retaking of the South Korean capital.

◀ **With fighting raging around the compound, U.S. Marine Corps Private Luther "Lee" Leguire raises the U.S. flag over the American consulate in Seoul on September 27, 1950. Not long after, Leguire was wounded in the knee by a Chinese bullet.**

▲ **The building is now the official residence of the U.S. ambassador to South Korea. The original building, purchased in 1908, was extensively damaged during the Korean War. Rebuilt in 1974, the building was renamed Habib House after the incumbent ambassador, Philip C. Habib.**

IMJIN RIVER
PAJU, SOUTH KOREA, APRIL 1951

Imjin River was the scene of a heroic battle fought between British and Chinese troops in the second year of the Korean War. When UN forces pushed north toward the 38th parallel, they established a front along the river, guarding the route to the South Korean capital, Seoul. The Chinese 63rd Army launched a counterattack and, on April 22, they crossed the river in strength. The British 29th Brigade was tasked with stopping the assault on Seoul. Supported by artillery and aircraft dropping napalm, the British soldiers beat back the enemy time and time again.

However, with no hope of relief, the order was given to withdraw. One unit, a battalion from the British Gloucestershire Regiment, had started the battle with 657 men. Only 63 reached safety. The Chinese had suffered 11,000 casualties during the battle and were forced to abandon the advance on Seoul.

◀ **The Freedom Bridge over the Imjin River, destroyed in 1951 to prevent the Chinese from using it. A replacement bridge can be seen in the foreground.**

▼ **The Freedom Bridge today, in Busan, South Korea. The Imjin River is nicknamed "River of the Dead" in the south, supposedly due to North Korean corpses seen floating in it as a result of starvation in the north during famines in the 1990s.**

1955—1975
VIETNAM WAR

MEKONG DELTA
VIETNAM, JANUARY 1961

Alarmed at the spread of communism throughout Southeast Asia, in 1961, U.S. President John F. Kennedy pledged military aid to South Vietnam, and by the end of that year there were 3,205 U.S. military personnel in the country. In large parts of South Vietnam, the government had lost control to the guerrillas of the Viet Cong (VC) waging an insurgency war against the authorities. The situation was especially acute in the Mekong Delta in the south of the country. Covering 26,000 square miles, the delta is flat and very fertile, being especially suited to growing rice. The huge number of rivers, canals, and

streams were ideal for the movement of small-scale VC units, against which the Army of the Republic of Vietnam (ARVN) had no answer. With the help of U.S. military advisers and equipment, however, the government began to fight back in the Mekong Delta. Eventually, the Americans would create the Mobile Riverine Force to combat the VC in the delta, working in conjunction with South Vietnamese army and marine units.

◀ **South Vietnamese and U.S. soldiers battling the VC in the Mekong Delta. American aid on the ground was organized by the U.S. Military Assistance Advisory Group Vietnam (MAAG-Vietnam). In the delta, American troops organized ambushes and attacks on enemy supply lines.**

▼ **The Mekong Delta today, much as it was during the war. The terrain is ideal for guerrilla warfare. VC insurgents could lie in wait in the trees and ambush government forces. The trees made aerial reconnaissance difficult, while the waterways allowed rapid exit from combat zones.**

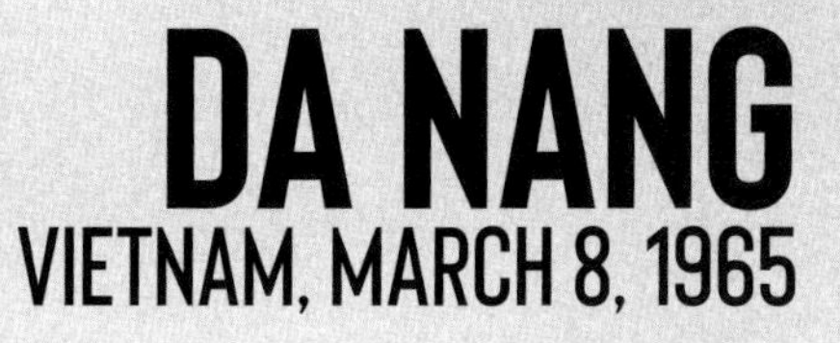

DA NANG

VIETNAM, MARCH 8, 1965

By 1965, the Viet Cong were attacking American installations throughout South Vietnam. In retaliation, President Lyndon B. Johnson sanctioned air strikes against North Vietnamese targets. In a highly symbolic move, the first U.S. combat force arrived in South Vietnam on March 8, 1965, with the 9th Marine Expeditionary Brigade landing at Da Nang, a city in Quang Nam province. The Americans would build a major port and airfield at Da Nang. It was a visual display of America's commitment, though the Joint Chiefs of Staff stressed that the Marines "will not engage in day-to-day actions against the Viet Cong." That stance would change in the months to come.

◀ Marines of the 9th Marine Expeditionary Brigade land on Da Nang beach on March 8. They were met on the beach by General Thi, commander of I Corps Tactical Zone, as well as the mayor of Da Nang and young women with garlands of flowers. The brigade comprised two battalions, one of which landed by air at Da Nang.

▼ With gentle slopes, the beach at Da Nang was ideal for amphibious landings. Close to the city, Da Nang's beaches are clean, picturesque, and popular destinations for both locals and tourists.

KHE SANH

VIETNAM, JANUARY 1968

During the Tet Offensive launched in January 1968, 20,000 North Vietnamese soldiers attacked the U.S. 26th Marine Regiment in Khe Sanh Combat Base, which was close to the Ho Chi Minh Trail, North Vietnam's main supply route to South Vietnam. The base's garrison numbered 6,000 men. It was attacked with fury on January 31, infantry and artillery pounding Marine positions on the high ground surrounding the base. Close to the border, the base was shelled by artillery in Laos as well as artillery and mortars closer to the Marines. The bombardment intensified throughout February. North Vietnamese infantry launched constant assaults against the base and the surrounding Marine hilltop strongpoints, which were repulsed with heavy losses. Two things saved Khe Sanh from being overrun: the failure of the North Vietnamese to capture the hills around the base, and total American air superiority. The siege finally ended on April 1, by which time 205 Marines and an estimated 10,000 North Vietnamese had been killed.

◀ **U.S. Marines watch American aircraft pound enemy positions outside Khe Sanh from the shelter of their trenches. The helicopter is a Sikorsky UH-34D.**

▲ **Today, the former base is a museum containing aircraft, tanks, and artillery from the 1968 siege. Visitors can walk on the former runway and tour the remains of bunkers and trenches.**

HUE
VIETNAM, JANUARY 1968

The old imperial capital of Hue was attacked by the North Vietnamese Army (NVA) and Viet Cong (VC) forces during the Tet Offensive. The city did not have a garrison, only a South Vietnamese company, which resulted in the NVA controlling all the Citadel (the Old City) and New City, aside from the company headquarters, by January 31. A relief force from the U.S. 1st Marine Regiment and South Vietnamese Army began to fight its way into the city. Hand-to-hand fighting—especially in the Citadel, where buildings were tightly packed together—raged until February 24, when Hue was finally cleared of NVA and VC forces.

▶ **The shattered remains of one entrance to the Citadel after the fighting had ended in Hue. The Citadel, where two-thirds of the people lived, was encompassed by miles of high walls with moats outside them.**

▶ **Many of the gates and buildings in the Citadel still bear bullet holes and other war damage from the fighting in January and February 1968. More than 80 percent of Hue's buildings were damaged in the battle for the city.**

▲ U.S. Marines outside the Meridian Gate during the fighting in Hue. The gate gave access to the Imperial Palace Compound, a walled city located at the southern end of the Citadel. Surrounded by 25-foot-high walls, the Palace Compound was a defender's dream.

▲ Both the Meridian Gate and the Imperial Palace were badly damaged during the battle for the city. Their restoration began in 1970 and continued under the communist regime.

HO CHI MINH CITY

VIETNAM, APRIL 1975

Following the Paris Peace Accords of 1973, the United States withdrew its ground forces from Vietnam. Two years later, the North Vietnamese Army (NVA) began an offensive against South Korea, aimed at the capture of Saigon, its capital. The Army of the Republic of Vietnam (ARVN) put up some resistance but then collapsed as NVA units approached the capital. Realizing the situation was hopeless, U.S. ambassador Graham Martin, with Washington's authorization, began Operation Frequent Wind, the evacuation of all American citizens from Saigon, at 11:08 a.m. on April 29. By the morning of the next day, the NVA had taken control of Saigon, subsequently renamed Ho Chi Minh City.

◀◀ One of the most iconic images of the Vietnam War. Americans, South Vietnamese, and other foreign nationals are evacuated from the Pittman Building, a CIA residential complex, in Saigon.

◀ The building at 22 Ly Tu Trong Street in downtown Ho Chi Minh City has hardly changed since 1975. It is not a tourist site as such, but visitors can take an elevator to visit the roof.

◀ An NVA tank and infantry pass the Notre Dame Cathedral of Saigon on April 30, 1975. Built by the French in the nineteenth century, the fact that the city fell without a fight meant the building suffered no war damage.

UNIFICATION PALACE Originally built as a residence for the governor-general of French Indochina in the nineteenth century and called the Norodom Palace, after the departure of the French following their defeat at Dien Bien Phu in 1954, the building was renamed the Independence Palace by the South Vietnamese government. In 1962, the building was damaged by military aircraft in an attempted coup. It was rebuilt using a design by the Vietnamese architect Ngo Viet Thu. His creation is the building that still stands in Ho Chi Minh City today, having opened in 1967. It was the residence of the South Vietnamese president until 1975.

▲ Left: A few minutes before 11:00 a.m. on April 30, 1975, a T-54 tank commanded by Lieutenant Vu Dang Toan smashed through the main gates of the palace compound and advanced on the building. Thirty minutes later, the red Communist banner was flying over the palace. The conference for national reconciliation was held in the palace later that year. Right: The palace is now a popular tourist destination.

▶ Top: NVA soldiers and tanks watch over palace staff captured on April 30. Quickly renamed the Reunification Palace, the building was not damaged by gunfire or explosions, despite being surrounded by tanks. A replica of the tank that crashed through the main gates of the palace on that day is now parked on the lawn in front of the palace. Bottom: Now primarily a tourist destination, the building is still occasionally used for official government functions.

INDEX

PICTURE CREDITS

The publisher would like to thank the following for the permission to reproduce copyrighted material.

Alamy: AB Forces News Collection: 111 (bottom); Album: 114; Alex's Pictures: 77 (bottom); Alpha Stock: 21 (top); Hans Blossey: 127 (top); Chon Kit Leong: 129; Chronicle: 126; Danita Delimont: 81 (right), 149; dpa picture alliance: 64, 105 (bottom); Eric Franks:13; Everett Collection Inc: 11 (top right), 144y; Granger Historical Picture Archive: 23 (center), Historical Images Archive: 38 (left); BRIAN HARRIS: 43, 48 (right); Hemis: 3, 51; INTERFOTO: 88 (top left); Ivy Close Images: 46; Jason Meyer: 25 (top); Ian Nellist: 38 (right); KGPA Ltd / Alamy Stock Photo: 28; The Print Collector: 42; The Protected Art Archive: 24 (top); Profimedia.CZ a.s.: 93 (bottom); REUTERS: 103; Boaz Rottem:133; Andrew Russell/Everett Collection Inc: front cover; Maurice Savage: 45 (bottom right); Science History Images: 132; Shawshots: 77 (top), 116; SPUTNIK: 89 (top); Stocktrek Images, Inc.: 106; Sueddeutsche Zeitung Photo: 2, 56 (top), 57 (top); Mark Summerfield: 23 (bottom); SuperStock: 94; Ken Welsh: 35; Westend61 GmbH: 67 (top), 107; World History Archive: 102; Agencja Fotograficzna Car: 117.

Australian War Memorial: 92

City of Vancouver Archives: Matthews, James Skitt, Major: 40 (top).

Dreamstime: Bozhdb: 87; Hernanhyper: 145; Lunfengzhe: 59 (bottom); Vandmc: 91.

William Mark Dyer: 10 (top right).

Getty: AFP: 130, 142–3, 146, 152, 155 (top); Sergey Alimov: 76 (bottom); Archive Holdings Inc.: 7; Archive Photos: 88; Bettmann: 104, 124, 142, 146, 152; Broderick/Stringer: 58 (bottom); Central Press: 150; Daily Herald Archive: 34 (top), 44 (top); DE AGOSTINI PICTURE LIBRARY: 85; Education Images: 101 (top), 154 (right); Fotosearch: 20 (top); FRANCE PRESSE VOIR/AFP; 62 (top); Galerie Bilderwelt: 100; Sean Gallup: 49 (bottom), 115; Herve GLOAGUEN: 153 (bottom left), 154 (left); Hulton Archive: 59 (top right), 118 (bottom left), 119 (center), 122; Hulton Deutsch: 30, 34, 60; HUM Images: 48 (left); Imperial War Museum: 50, 66, 98; Keystone-France: 45 (top); Keystone/Staff: 67 (bottom center); Silvana Leinung: 113; Peter Macdiarmid: 39 (bottom); Ernest Brooks/Mirrorpix: 24–5; Mirrorpix: 26, 31 (top), 156; Mondadori Portfolio: 59 (center), 84; Nine OK: 19 (top), ; NurPhoto: 101 (bottom); George Pachantouris: 62 (bottom); Douglas Peebles: 79; Picture alliance: 82; Berliner Verlag/Archiv/picture alliance: 63 (top); Pictures from History: 80; Serge Plantureux: 74; Popperfoto; 45 (bottom left); Bentley Archive/ Popperfoto: 68, 70 (top); Bob Thomas/Popperfoto: 32 (bottom); Print Collector: 17 (centre), 32 (top); Raymond Kleboe Collection: 96 (top); Mark Redkin: 118 (top); Ullstein bild Dtl.: 90, 120; Universal History Archive: 58 (top); Flavio Vallenari: 29; Roger Viollet: 36; Windmill Books: 39 (top).

Wayne Hsieh: 119 (top).

istockphotos: BackyardProduction: 11 (bottom right); catnap72: 21 (bottom); Jotily; 125; Steve Loncto: 8–9; lucentius: 31 (bottom); NgKhanhVuKhoa: 151 (top and bottom right); Quangpraha: 153 (bottom right); Erik V; 65; Lisa Valder: 61; Eli Wilson: 17 (top).

Library of Congress: George N. Barnard, Brady/Liljenquist Family collection, LC-DIG-ppmsca-66661: 10 (top left); Russell, Andrew J./Brady Handy Collection/National Archives, LC-DIG-ppmsca-34851: 12; Gardner, Alexander, 1821-1882, LC-DIG-cwpb-00307: 14 (top); Gardner, Alexander, 1821-1882/LOC 2018666235: 15 (top right); Gardner, Alexander, 1821-1882, LC-B811- 2384: 18; LC-B8172-1757: 19 (bottom); LC-DIG-ppmsca-35111: 22 (top); O'Sullivan, Timothy H., 1840-1882, LC-DIG-cwpb-00348: 23 (top); LC-USZ61-903: 25 (top left).

Mary Evans: Westernfrontphotography.com: 44 (bottom).

National Archives of Canada: PA-148880/Cdn. Govt. Motion Pict. Bureau/National Film Board of Canada. Photothèque: 41 (top).

Shutterstock: Bayurov Alexander: 88 (bottom); AP: 52 (top and bottom), 53 (top and bottom), 71 (top), 108; Eddie Adams/AP: 151 (top and bottom left); Rick Merron/AP: 148; Joe Rosenthal/AP: 54, 111 (top), 158; Timothy L Barnes: 24 (bottom); Jon Bilous: 15 (bottom right); Joey Cheung: 70 (bottom); Chrislofotos: 41 (bottom); Ciwoa: 99, 109 (top); Dimbar76: 75; Erik AJV: 63 (bottom); Efired: 150 (bottom); Everett Collection: 96 (bottom), 110; EWY Media: 17 (bottom); f11photo: 131; Wolfgang Hauke: 121; Karovka: 89 (bottom); LeQuangNhut: 155 (bottom); Mateusz Kuca: 97; Malachi Jacobs: 14 (bottom); Marcin Krzyzak: 93 (top right); Mateusz Kuca: 97; Maziarz: 71 (bottom); milosk50: 33 (top); Nagel Photography: 20 (bottom); Northcliffe Collection/ANL: 112; Marek Poplawski: 2, 56 (bottom), 57 (bottom); Francesco Ricciardi Exp: 73 (top); Stock for you: 137; Tang Trung Kien: 147; Todamo: 40 (bottom); Trabantos: 123, 141; Michael Tubi: 69; Underworld: 95.

U.S. National Archives: ID 526067: 17 (middle right); ID 531005: 49 (top); ID 541899: 67 (bottom left): ID 195617: 78; ID 531170: 93 (top left); ID 292569: 105 (top); ID 532379: 128.

Unsplash: Johen Redman: 7; Murilo Silva: 83 (top); Francesco Zivoli: 118 (bottom right), 119 (bottom).

Wikimedia Commons: Australian War Memorial: 33; Photo studio E. Bieber: 47 (left); German Federal Archives: 83; François GOGLINS: 47 (right); Nate Kornegay/Creative Commons CC by 2.0: 139; U.S. National Archives: 134–5, 136; U.S. National Archives 531427: 140; U.S. National Archives/Imperial Japanese Navy: 81 (top left); U.S. National Archives/Timothy H. O'Sullivan: 16; Review of Reviews Co: 25 (top right); RIA Novosti archive, image #887721/Knorring/ CC-BY-SA 3.0: 76 (top); Nic Saigon: 153 (top); Sergey Strunnikov: 86; U.S. Marines (Official Marine Corps Photo # A3386): 138; Arthur Conry/Wiki-Ed: 72.

While every effort has been made to credit photographers, The Bright Press would like to apologize should there have been any omissions or errors, and would be pleased to make the appropriate correction for future editions of the book.